The Jacobit

NEW FRONTIERS IN HISTORY

series editors
Mark Greengrass
Department of History, Sheffield University
John Stevenson
Worcester College, Oxford

This important new series reflects the substantial expansion that has occurred in the scope of history syllabuses. As new subject areas have emerged and syllabuses have come to focus more upon methods of historical enquiry and knowledge of source materials, a growing need has arisen for correspondingly broad-ranging textbooks.

New Frontiers in History provides up-to-date overviews of key topics in British, European and world history, together with accompanying source material and appendices. Authors focus upon subjects where revisionist work is being undertaken, providing a fresh viewpoint which will be welcomed by students and sixth-formers. The series also explores established topics which have attracted much conflicting analysis and require a synthesis of the state of the debate.

Published Titles

C. J. Bartlett Defence and diplomacy: Britain and the Great Powers, 1815–1914

Jeremy Black The politics of Britain, 1688–1800

Keith Laybourn The General Strike of 1926

Forthcoming titles

Paul Bookbinder The Weimar Republic

Joanna Bourke Production and reproduction: working women in Britain, 1860–1960

Michael Braddick The nerves of state: taxation and the financing of the English state, 1558–1714

Ciaran Brady The unplanned conquest: social changes and political conflict in sixteenth-century Ireland

David Brooks The age of upheaval: Edwardian politics, 1899–1914

David Carlton Churchill and the Soviets

Carl Chinn Poverty and the urban poor in the nineteenth century

Barry Coward The Cromwellian Protectorate

Conan Fischer The rise of the Nazis

Neville Kirk The rise of Labour, 1850–1920

Tony Kushner The Holocaust and its aftermath

Alan O'Day Irish Home Rule

Panikos Panayi Immigrants, minorities and British society, 1815–1919

John Whittam Fascist Italy

The Jacobites
Britain and Europe
1688–1788

Daniel Szechi

Manchester University Press
Manchester and New York
Distributed exclusively in the USA and Canada by St. Martin's Press

Published by Manchester University Press
Oxford Road, Manchester M13 9PL, UK
and Room 400, 175 Fifth Avenue, New York, NY 10010, USA

Distributed exclusively in the USA and Canada by St. Martin's Press, Inc.,
175 Fifth Avenue, New York, NY 10010, USA

British Library Cataloguing-in-Publication Data
A catalogue record for this book is available from the British Library

Library of Congress Cataloging-in-Publication Data

Szechi, D. (Daniel)
  The Jacobites, Britain, and Europe, 1688–1788/Daniel Szechi.
    p.   cm. — (New frontiers in History)
  Includes bibliographical reference and index.
  ISBN 0–7190–3773–5. — ISBN 0–7190–3774–3 (pbk.)
    1. Great Britain—History—18th century. 2. Great Britain—
History—William and Mary, 1689–1702. 3. Great Britain—History—
Revolution of 1688. 4. Great Britain—Foreign relations—Europe.
5. Europe—Foreign relations—Great Britain. 6. Jacobites.
I. Title. II. Series
DA480.S94   1994
941.07—dc20   93–27931
                                                                            CIP

ISBN 0 7190 3773 5 *hardback*
     0 7190 3774 3 *paperback*

Reprinted in paperback in 1996

Typeset by The Midlands Book Typesetting Company, Loughborough
Printed in Great Britain by Bell and Bain Ltd, Glasgow

For Jan, in the hope that she will read this

Contents

General editors' preface

The history of England under the Hanoverians has often been written from the perspective of the successful – both politically and socially. The great age of Whig supremacy consolidated more than a political system or a society; it created a view of itself and its past which historians have come to know as a 'Whig' interpretation of the past. In another contribution to this series, Jeremy Black has already outlined the greater complexities of Britain's political history in this period as they are coming to be understood by historians.* Now Daniel Szechi analyses the ways in which 'Hanoverian' history can be seen through a 'Jacobite' lens. Historians often do not like writing about failures, glorious or otherwise. Szechi properly reminds us of the ways in which things might have turned out very differently for the Jacobites as a means for us to understand more clearly the underlying realities of events as they actually happened. He does so in a broader British and European perspective and, as a result, suggests the ways in which Jacobitism has come to be understood and interpreted more positively by historians.

Mark Greengrass
John Stevenson

* Jeremy Black, *The politics of britain, 1688–1800*, New Frontiers in History Series, Manchester U.P., 1993.

Author's acknowledgements

For permission to publish extracts and citations in this book I am indebted to: Her Majesty the Queen for her gracious permission to use the Stuart Papers microfilm owned by the Ralph Brown Draughon Library, Auburn University; the Scottish Catholic Archives for the use of the Blair Letters; Mrs C. Methuen Campbell for the use of the Penrice and Margam collection held at the National Library of Wales. My thanks are also due to the staff of the Bodleian Library, Oxford, and the National Library of Scotland for their courtesy and patience.

In addition, I must thank the RBD Library at Auburn for diverting a substantial chunk of their gift fund into buying a copy of the Stuart Papers microfilm for me to consult, and, as well, my colleagues in the History Department who unanimously voted to mortgage our department's annual library budget to cover the rest of the cost. I have a special debt of gratitude to my former colleague Bob Rea for reading and commenting on an early draught of this book at a time when he had little leisure to do so, and to Paul Monod, who took time off from enjoying the company of his new-born son to offer some lively, and very helpful, criticism. None of the above is in any way to blame for the crudeness and infelicities that follow; they are all my responsibility.

Abbreviations

HMC	Historical Manuscripts Commission
ns	New style date
Stuart Papers	Ralph Brown Draughon Library, Auburn University Library, Stuart Papers microfilm

The place of publication of all works cited in the notes and bibliography is London unless otherwise stated.

Note on dates

The British Isles remained on the Julian calendar until 1751, which put Britain's calendar 10 days behind Continental Europe in the seventeenth century and 11 days in the eighteenth. Unless otherwise noted, all dates are given in the old style, Julian Calendar, though it is assumed that each new year began on 1 January rather than 25 March. Where new style, Gregorian Calendar, dates are cited they are denoted by an 'ns' following the date in question.

A Jacobite chronology

1688

10 Jun.	Birth of James Francis Edward, Prince of Wales
5 Nov.	William of Orange lands at Torbay
10 Dec.	Mary of Modena escapes to France with the Prince of Wales
23 Dec.	James II escapes to France

1689

28 Jan.	House of Commons declares James II to have abdicated the throne by his flight
12 Mar.	James II lands at Kinsale in Ireland with 5,000 French troops
25 Mar.	Scottish Convention declares the throne 'forfaulted'
18 Apr.	James II fired on by the defenders of Londonderry; formal siege of city begins
1 May	Royal Navy squadron defeated at battle of Bantry Bay
7 May	Revanchist Catholic 'Patriot Parliament' meets in Dublin
18 May	Dundee musters Jacobite clans at Lochaber and launches the Highland War
17 Jul.	Dundee routs Mackay's Williamites at Killiecrankie, but is killed in process
28 Jul.	Royal Navy breaks through to relieve the starving defenders of Londonderry

13 Aug.	Duke of Schomberg and a Williamite army land at Carrickfergus
21 Aug.	Cannon's Scots Jacobite army repulsed by Cameronians at Dunkeld

1690

1 Feb.	Over 400 Anglican clergy (including 5 bishops) deprived for refusing the oaths to William and Mary; beginning of Nonjuror schism
1 May	Buchan's Scots Jacobite army routed at the Haughs of Cromdale; guerilla war commences in Highlands
7 Jun.	Presbyterianism officially re-established in Scotland; beginning of Scots Episcopalian schism
30 Jun.	Anglo-Dutch fleet defeated at Beachy head
1 Jul.	William III defeats James II at the Boyne
3 Jul.	James II leaves Ireland for France
30 Aug.	William III forced to raise first siege of Limerick and retreat to Dublin

1691

1 Jan.	Preston captured *en route* to St Germain; subsequently reveals details of Jacobite plotting
30 Jun.	Breadalbane negotiates truce in Highland War while Jacobite clans seek James II's permission to negotiate surrender
12 Jul.	Ginkel's Williamite army defeats French and Jacobites under St Ruth at Aughrim
3 Oct.	Limerick surrenders on generous terms; most of garrison opt to be evacuated to France
2 Dec.	James II gives Jacobite clans permission to surrender

1692

Jan.	Jacobite clans surrender to the government
13 Feb.	Massacre of Macdonalds of Glencoe
19–20 May	Anglo-Dutch fleet scatters French at Barfleur; subsequently corners and burns French stragglers at La Hogue (23–4 May); projected Franco-Jacobite invasion abandoned
18 Jun.	Birth of Princess Louisa Maria Theresa ('la consolatrix')

1693

c. 1 Apr.   Middleton arrives in France to take up position as Jacobite co-Secretary of State with Melfort and Caryll

7 Apr.   James II issues Protestant-oriented manifesto

1694

16 May   James II dismisses Melfort

17–22 Oct.   8 prominent Lancashire Catholics acquitted of Jacobite conspiracy (the 'Lancashire Plot')

1695

Oct.   Preparations begin for coordinated French invasion and Jacobite rising known as the Fenwick plot

1696

Jan.   Faction among Jacobite conspirators in England hatch Assassination plot

15 Feb.   Authorities alerted to Jacobite conspiracy by Assassination plot informers

22 Feb.   Mass arrests of Jacobite conspirators begin

Mar.–Apr.   7 Jacobite conspirators tried and executed; 5 more condemned to life imprisonment without trial by Act of Parliament

c. 1 May   French invasion plan abandoned

c. Jun.   Onset of 4 years of famine in Scotland ('King William's ill years')

23 Dec.   Fenwick condemned to death by Act of Attainder

1697

10 Sep.   Peace of Ryswick; Louis XIV recognises William III as King of England; James II spurns secret offer by William III to raise Prince of Wales as his heir

1700

c. Aug.   Melfort returns to St Germain

1701

17 Feb.   Parliament votes funds to rearm fleet after Melfort letter revealing Jacobite conspiracy intercepted; French government exiles Melfort to Angers

24 Apr.	Act of Succession designating the House of Hanover as William III and Princess Anne's heirs
6 Sep.	Death of James II; Louis XIV recognises Old Pretender as 'James III'
Nov.–Jan. 1702	Belhaven fails to persuade Mary of Modena to allow the Old Pretender to be brought up in Scotland (as a Protestant)

1702

7 Mar.	Abjuration Act requiring formal renunciation of allegiance to the Old Pretender
8 Mar.	Death of William III; accession of Queen Anne
Aug.	Middleton converts to Catholicism and briefly retires from office

1703

May–Oct.	Simon Fraser, 'Lord' Lovat, concocts fake ('Scotch') plot in Highlands

1704

17 Jan.	Lovat incarcerated in Paris for his role in the Scotch plot
3 Aug.	Eugene and Marlborough decisively defeat Franco-Bavarian army at Blenheim

1705

Aug.–Sep.	Hooke reconnoitres Scotland to assess seriousness of Jacobite pledges of support

1706

Oct.–Dec.	Passage of Act of Union in Scotland; Jacobites plan uprising but are let down by Hamilton

1707

Apr.–Sep.	Hooke returns to Scotland to plan rebellion with Jacobite leaders

1708

c. 1 Feb.	British government receives first warning of French invasion
27 Feb.	Old Pretender arrives at Dunkirk but comes down with measles; Royal Navy squadron arrives off Dunkirk same day

6 Mar.	French expedition under Forbin evades Royal Navy and sails for Scotland
12 Mar.	Expedition arrives in Firth of Forth, but misses Jacobite pilots and signals; Forbin insists on turning back despite pleas of Old Pretender

1710

27 Feb.–20 Mar.	Impeachment of High Church divine, Henry Sacheverell, provokes serious rioting in London and elsewhere
Sep.	Jersey, negotiating terms of a separate peace with French agent on behalf of Harley ministry, asserts it is willing to restore the Old Pretender
Sep.–Oct.	c. 332 Tories are returned in electoral landslide precipitated by Sacheverell impeachment

1711

Jan.	High Tory and Jacobite 'October Club' of backbenchers makes its first appearance in the Commons
27 Sep.	Preliminary articles for a (separate) peace with France made public by the Harley ministry
Oct.–Nov.	Elector of Hanover (future George I) makes clear his displeasure at ministry's proceedings

1712

18 Aug.	Princess Louisa dies of smallpox at St Germain

1713

18 Feb.	Old Pretender leaves France for Lorraine
3 May	Oxford requests Old Pretender order his followers in Britain to support the ministry in the upcoming election; Old Pretender agrees
13 Dec.	Middleton resigns as Jacobite Secretary of State
24–8 Dec.	Queen Anne briefly, but seriously, ill

1714

15 Jan.	Oxford demands Old Pretender convert to Protestantism before he will seek to restore him
6 Feb.	Bolingbroke, independently demands Old Pretender's conversion as a prerequisite for action
2 Mar.	Old Pretender refuses to contemplate conversion
21 Jun.	Cabinet agrees to post reward of £5,000 (subsequently increased by vote in Commons to

	£100,000) for apprehension of Old Pretender in the event of his landing in Britain
22 Jun.–c.4 Jul.	Jacobite MPs begin harrassing ministerial supply bills
c.5 Jul.	Bolingbroke promises to work to restore Old Pretender; Jacobite obstruction of supply ceases
1 Aug.	Queen Anne dies; George I peacefully proclaimed throughout British Isles
10 Aug.	Old Pretender arrives incognito in Paris seeking French help; Louis XIV sends him back to Lorraine
Oct.	Wave of High Tory rioting against Dissenters sweeps Midlands and southern England; George I crowned (20th)

1715

Jan.	Whigs win crushing electoral victory
26 Mar.	Bolingbroke flees to France
12–21 Jun.	Oxford, Bolingbroke, Ormond and Strafford impeached
Jun.–Aug.	Intense wave of pro-Jacobite rioting sweeps Midlands and north of England
12 Jul.	Bolingbroke appointed Jacobite Secretary of State
1 Aug.	Earl of Mar returns to Scotland and retires to the Highlands
8 Aug.	Ormond flees to France
21 Aug.	death of Louis XIV; Orléans becomes Regent
6 Sep.	Mar raises standard of rebellion at Braemar
14 Sep.	Hay captures Perth for the Jacobites
6 Oct.	Forster and Derwentwater proclaim the Old Pretender on Waterfalls Hill in Northumberland
11 Oct.	Kenmuir musters Lowland Jacobites at Moffat
12–13 Oct.	Borlum's Macintoshes cross the Firth of Forth
19 Oct.	Kenmuir and Forster link up at Rothbury
22 Oct.	Borlum reaches Kelso and links up with Forster and Kenmuir
28 Oct.	Failing to receive the expected signals Ormond abandons attempt to land in West Country and sails back to France

2 Nov.	Forster et al. reach Penrith, routing *posse-comitatus* en route
7 Nov.	Forster reaches Lancaster; flow of Jacobite recruits steps up
9–10 Nov.	Forster moves into Preston; Mar marches south
12 Nov.	Kenmuir and Borlum barricade Preston; Wills attempts to storm town and is bloodily repulsed; Mar advances towards Dunblane; Argyll advances from Stirling onto Sherrifmuir
13 Nov.	Forster's Jacobites repulse another attack; Carpenter reinforces Wills; Forster decides to surrender; Mar and Argyll draw battle at Sherrifmuir
14 Nov.	Forster's army surrenders; Mar retreats to Perth
22 Dec.	Old Pretender lands at Peterhead near Aberdeen
1716	
23 Jan.	Old Pretender crowned James VIII of Scotland at Perth
31 Jan.	Jacobite army retreats from Perth in the face of Argyll's advance northwards
4 Feb.	Old Pretender and Mar depart for France
8 Feb.	Main Jacobite force disperses
c. 12 Feb.	Old Pretender dismisses Bolingbroke
11 Mar.	Mar appointed Jacobite Secretary of State
23 Mar.	Jacobite court retreats to Avignon
Jun.–Jul.	Fighting in London between Jacobites and Whig 'Mug-house' gangs
Aug.	Negotiations with Sweden for an invasion (the Swedish plot) commence at Paris
17 Nov.	Anglo-French alliance signed
1717	
25 Jan.	Old Pretender departs from Avignon
29 Jan.	Swedish Ambassador in London arrested; 'Swedish' plot aborted
Feb.	Jacobite court settles at Urbino
Jun.–Mar. 1718	Ormond negotiations with Peter the Great
1718	
28 Apr.	Death of Queen Mary of Modena
11 Aug.	Anglo-Dutch fleet decisively defeats Spanish fleet off Cape Passaro

Sep.	Clementina Sobieska, en route to wed the Old Pretender, arrested by Charles VI at Innsbruck
Oct.	Preparations for a Spanish invasion of England, supported by a Jacobite rising (the "19'), commence
6 Dec.	Britain declares war on Spain

1719

24 Feb.	Main Spanish invasion force (aimed at England) sails from Cadiz
25 Feb.	Secondary Spanish invasion force (aimed at Scotland) sails from Los Pasajes
13 Mar.	Mar resigns as Jacobite Secretary of State
18 Mar.	Main Spanish expedition dispersed by storm; invasion plan abandoned
9 Apr.	Marischal and 2 ships reach Lewis
17 Apr.	Clementina escapes from Innsbruck
5 Jun.	Marischal and Scots Jacobite army defeated at Glenshiel by a force under Wightman
22 Aug.	Old Pretender marries Clementina Sobieska
Oct.	Jacobite court moves to Rome

1720

Feb.–Aug.	South Sea Bubble crisis
20 Dec.	Birth of Charles Edward Stuart

1721

Oct.	Genesis of conspiracy known as the Atterbury plot

1722

May–Sep.	Ministry systematically arrests most of 'Atterbury' plotters
27 Nov.	Layer convicted of treason

1723

6–15 May	Bill of pains and penalties passed against Atterbury
17 May	Layer executed
18 Jun.	Atterbury leaves England for exile in France
Oct.	Renewed negotiations with Peter the Great
21 Nov.	Death of Orléans

1725

28 Jan.	Death of Peter the Great; end of negotiations with Russians

22 Feb.	Hay appointed Jacobite Secretary of State and created Earl of Inverness
23 Feb.	Birth of Henry Benedict Stuart
29 Apr.	Alliance of Vienna between Habsburgs and Spain
4 Nov.	Clementina withdraws to convent demanding dismissal of Hay

1726

Sep.	Old Pretender and Jacobite court withdraw to Bologna

1727

23 Mar.	Hay resigns and 'Sir' John Graeme replaces him as Jacobite Secretary of State
11 Jun.	Death of George I; George II succeeds peacefully
mid–Jun.	Old Pretender gallops (incognito) to Lorraine; Clementina emerges from convent and goes to Bologna
31 Jul.	Old Pretender obliged to quit Lorraine for Avignon
30 Sep.	Graeme dismissed as Jacobite Secretary of State; replaced by James Murray of Stormont ('Earl of Dunbar')
30 Dec.	Old Pretender returns to Bologna

1729

Apr.	Jacobite court returns to Rome

1730

11 Jan.	Old Pretender instructs his followers in Parliament to unite with any other opponents of ministry to bring down Walpole

1731

Jan.	Cornbury first contacts Jacobite court
22 Jul.	2nd treaty of Vienna between Britain and Habsburgs signals virtual end of Anglo-French alliance

1733

Mar.–May	Excise Crisis
Jun.	Cornbury plotters approach France for aid
Oct.–Nov.	Cornbury plot peters out due to French lack of interest

1735

7 Jan.	Death of Clementina Sobieska
30 Sep.	Outbreak of War of Polish Succession; Britain diplomatically isolated

1736

Sep.	Porteus riots in Edinburgh

1737

2 Dec.	Gordon of Glenbucket invites Old Pretender to send Charles Edward to Scotland with or without foreign support

1739

19 Oct.	Britain declares war on Spain

1740

May	Barrymore visits Paris on behalf of Jacobite Tory leadership to urge French to invade in name of Old Pretender
5 Dec.	Frederick the Great invades Silesia, sparking War of Austrian Succession

1741

16 Sep.	Old Pretender instructs Jacobite MPs and peers to cooperate with dissident Whigs to bring down Walpole

1742

6 Feb.	Walpole resigns
Mar.	Tories once more refused public office by George II; Pulteneyites abandon them to join ministry

1743

18 Jan.	Death of Cardinal Fleury
Aug.–Oct.	Butler scouts English Jacobite support for a French invasion
Nov.	French preparations for surprise attack on England begin
30 Dec.	Charles Edward commences secret journey to France

1744

14 Feb.	British government discovers plot; mass arrests follow
24 Feb.	French preparations wrecked by storm
28 Feb.	French shelve invasion plan
Aug.	Charles Edward begins secret preparations for an unsupported invasion and rising in Scotland

1745

30 Apr.	French defeat Cumberland's Anglo-Dutch army at Fontenoy
5 Jul.	Charles Edward sets sail from Nantes
23 Jul.	Charles Edward lands on Eriskay
19 Aug.	Jacobite standard raised at Glenfinnan
17 Sep.	Jacobite army captures Edinburgh
21 Sep.	Jacobites rout Cope's army at Prestonpans
8 Nov.	Jacobite army enters England on march south
Nov.	French commence invasion preparations
5 Dec.	Jacobite officers insist on army turning back at Derby
20 Dec.	Jacobite army re-enters Scotland
23–5 Dec.	Henry Benedict arrives at Boulogne, but French expedition fails to set out and is bottled up by Royal Navy

1746

17 Jan.	Jacobites defeat Hawley at Falkirk
1 Feb.	French invasion cancelled and forces redeployed; Jacobite army begins retreat to Highlands
16 Apr.	Jacobite army defeated at Culloden by Cumberland
17–20 Apr.	Jacobite army rallies at Ruthven; disperses on orders from Charles Edward
Apr.–Sep.	Cumberland harries Highlands; Charles Edward in hiding
30 Sep.	Charles Edward arrives back in France

1747

Jan.–Feb.	Charles Edward solicits support in Spain
19 Apr.	Henry Benedict flees Charles Edward; returns to Rome

22 Jun.	Henry Benedict enters Catholic church and is raised to cardinalate
22–9 Sep.	Jacobite demonstrations at Lichfield races

1748

18 Oct.	Peace of Aix-la-Chapelle ends War of Austrian Succession
30 Nov.	Charles Edward abducted on Louis XV's orders and incarcerated at Vincennes
3 Dec.	Charles Edward released on condition he leave France
16 Dec.	Charles Edward arrives in Avignon

1749

14 Feb.	Charles Edward departs from Avignon to begin peripatetic, disguised existence

1750

May–Jul.	Sustained Jacobite rioting in and around Walsall
5–12 Sep.	Charles Edward visits London to consult with English Jacobite leaders; while there is formally converted to Anglicanism

1751

Feb.	Frederick the Great meets Charles Edward in Berlin; genesis of Elibank plot

1752

May	Charles Edward resumes relationship with Clementina Walkinshaw despite English Jacobite objections
10–12 Jun.	Jacobite riots in Exeter

1753

Mar.	Elibank plot betrayed; Cameron captured preparing revolt in Highlands
7 Jun.	Cameron executed – last man to die for Jacobite cause
29 Oct.	Birth of Charlotte, Charles Edward's daughter by Clementina Walkinshaw

1754
Apr.   After acrimonious row between Marischal and Charles Edward, the English Jacobites sever all relations with him

1759
5 Feb.   Charles Edward meets Choiseul to discuss projected French invasion of England; Choiseul disgusted by his drunken obstinacy but continues preparations
20 Nov.   Royal Navy decisively defeats French fleet at Quiberon Bay, aborting planned invasion

1760
22 Jul.   Clementina Walkinshaw flees Charles Edward's drunken violence, taking her daughter with her
25 Oct.   Death of George II; George III peacefully succeeds

1766
1 Jan.   Death of the Old Pretender
14 Jan.   Pope Clement XIII formally refuses to acknowledge Charles Edward as King Charles 'III'

1772
17 Apr.   Charles Edward marries Louise von Stolberg

1774
Oct.   Jacobite court moves to Florence

1780
9 Dec.   Louise von Stolberg flees to a convent to escape Charles Edward's alcoholic violence

1783
Dec.   Gustav III of Sweden stays with Charles Edward in Florence

1784
Jun.   Charles Edward summons his daughter Charlotte, recognises and legitimises her

1785
Dec.   Jacobite court returns to Rome

1788

30 Jan.   Death of Charles Edward; Scots Episcopalian church ceases to pray for the exiled Stuarts

1789

17 Nov.   Death of Charlotte Walkinshaw

1804

Last known meeting of a Nonjuring congregation (in Manchester)

1807

13 Jul.   Death of Henry Benedict, last of James II's direct heirs

1

Introduction

Jacobitism is a fertile source of some of the great 'what-ifs' of British history. What if William of Orange had been killed at the battle of the Boyne in 1690? What if the Earl of Mar had crushed the Duke of Argyll's little army at the battle of Sherrifmuir in 1715? Most potent of all, what if Charles Edward Stuart (the Young Pretender) had not turned back at Derby in 1745? Of course we can never *know* the answers to any of these questions because history is not an experiment where one can adjust the variables and repeat the procedure. All historians can do is interpret the maddeningly imprecise data that has survived the vicissitudes of time. Nevertheless, Jacobitism's power to generate the 'what-ifs' so beloved of romantic novelists is instructive. The subject is an emotive one on which many other events in British history, such as the creation of a stable polity, the Union of Scotland and England, the onset of the industrial revolution, the rise of the first British empire, and so on, can be argued to hinge. This tantalising sense that Jacobitism had the potential to make the history of Britain turn out very differently has in turn resulted in some major divisions among historians of the eighteenth century. For the purposes of this introduction those whose work has been most significant for the historiography of Jacobitism is grouped under three headings: optimists, pessimists and rejectionists.

None of these labels should be taken as any reflection on the scholarship or theoretical methodology of the historians concerned. The sheer erudition of both Paul Hopkins's and Paul Langford's work, for example, is awesome, despite the fact that they are

1

poles apart in their interpretation of Jacobitism; and Marxisant historians like Frank McLynn can be found comfortably aligned on many historiographical issues with more conservative scholars such as Eveline Cruickshanks.[1] What follows is thus an attempt to create a shorthand categorisation of modern historians with respect to their attitude to the Jacobite phenomenon that students will find useful. It is worth noting here, too, that many other scholars have dealt with aspects of Jacobitism in their work – amongst others, Jeremy Black, Geoffrey Holmes and Sir John Plumb[2] – and the historians cited below as representative of the optimist, pessimist and rejectionist schools of interpretation are simply my idiosyncratic choice of voices from a lively, and continuing, debate.[3]

The optimists

'Optimism' in the sense used below, refers specifically to this school of historiography's attitude towards the seriousness of the Jacobite threat, not to a belief that anything especially beneficial to mankind might have come out of Jacobitism *per se*. In a sense, this school is directly descended from the romantic tradition of Jacobitism created by Sir Walter Scott at the beginning of the nineteenth century.[4] By then real Jacobitism was long dead, the monstrous caricatures of Hanoverian black propaganda thankfully forgotten, and from the vantage point of post-Napoleonic Britain it could safely be regarded sentimentally, even fondly by the ruling elite of the new, industrial Britain.[5]

From the mid-nineteenth century on there was an efflorescence of publishing on the subject of Jacobitism, most of it arguing strenuously for this or that event as the crucial turning point, but always with the underlying conviction that but for 'x' or 'y' happening, Bonnie Prince Charlie would have regained the throne of his ancestors. The only enduring contribution made to the field by this explosion of interest came in the form of the publication of a great many original documents by semi-antiquarian scholars, amongst whom Alastair and Henrietta Tayler stand out for the cool empiricism and quality of their editing.[6] Nonetheless, this renaissance of interest in Jacobitism did give rise to one fully coherent statement of the optimist case – in the work of Sir Charles Petrie. Petrie was a devout Roman Catholic, which undoubtedly coloured his judgement on occasion. Nevertheless, he argued powerfully in a series of articles and books that Jacobitism was a genuine political movement (in a twentieth-century sense), with a mass following, and that on several occasions it came within an ace of overthrowing the post-Revolutionary political order in the British Isles.[7]

Petrie's enthusiasm, however, sometimes overcame his scholarship,[8] and as a result the optimist school of thought – associated by Petrie with Cavalier reaction and paternalism – was increasingly marginalised after World War II as more and more professional historians turned to social history and cliometricism in various forms. By its very nature, Jacobitism, believed at the time to be an almost wholly elite movement, went against the *zeitgeist* of the historical community of the 1940s and 1950s. The optimist interpretation accordingly remained in the doldrums until 1970. In that year, the History of Parliament Trust brought out two volumes on the House of Commons 1715–54, which included an analysis of the Tory party's politics in that period primarily written by the then assistant editor Eveline Cruickshanks (later editor of the 1689–1715 volumes). These made a strong case for the Tory party's deep involvement in active Jacobitism, suggested that in 1743–5 the Tories were certainly ready to rise if a French invasion arrived and that they came within a whisker of doing so as Charles Edward marched south.[9] In 1979 Dr Cruickshanks backed up her argument with a book on the 1743–4 conspiracy which was primarily based on previously underused or overlooked French archival sources.[10]

Her case was reinforced in 1981 by Frank McLynn's book on the French response to the '45, in which he proved that the French did their level best to assemble an invasion force for southern England designed to link up with Charles Edward's army on its way south, and only missed him by a narrow margin.[11] In the mid-1980s Paul Hopkins added to the weight of the optimists' gathering reassessment of the Jacobite phenomenon by conclusively proving that the Highland war of 1689–91 was not the unimportant little episode most historians had previously considered it to be, but rather a crippling civil war that bankrupted the post-Revolutionary Scottish state morally and financially.[12] To round off an exciting decade for the optimist school, Paul Monod's pioneering study of the social history of Jacobitism strongly suggested there was a lot of popular support for the Jacobite cause amongst the lower as well as the upper orders of English society, and that its ideology enjoyed widespread acceptance at all levels.[13]

The pessimists

The pessimist school of Jacobite historiography takes a reserved position about the seriousness of the Jacobite threat. In general, its exponents do not deny the importance of Jacobitism in the development of the British polity, nor of its long-term impact on European diplomacy. The crucial point on which they consistently differ with the optimists is in their evaluation of the power of inertia, the Revolution settlement and the British state to hold the Jacobites at bay and ultimately to defeat them. The most wide-ranging, empirical statement of the pessimist case to date was published by George Hilton Jones in 1954. Jones considered the subject from a mainly diplomatic perspective, and put forward an interpretation that viewed the Jacobites as self-deluding tools of their erstwhile backers with correspondingly little prospect of success.[14] As far as academic historians were concerned, Jones completely superseded Petrie and was considered to have said the last word on the subject.

Consequently little further work was done on Jacobitism by historians of the pessimist school until the early 1970s, when Edward Gregg began publishing articles that challenged long-held assumptions on various subjects relating to Jacobitism, most notably that Queen Anne was sympathetic to the idea of a second restoration. In one devastating article, later backed up at length in a full dress biographical reassessment of the queen, Gregg conclusively killed the notion that she ever wished to restore her half-brother, James Francis Edward Stuart (the Old Pretender).[15] Gregg's revitalisation of the pessimist interpretation was trenchantly reinforced in the mid-1970s by Paul Fritz's careful dissection of the way Walpole manipulated the political nation's fear of Jacobitism to serve his own political ends, and the late Gareth Bennett's reassessment of the career and motivation of one of the most notorious of Jacobite plotters: Francis Atterbury, Bishop of Rochester.[16] More agnostic, but overall still pessimist, analyses by Bruce Lenman of the nature of Scottish Jacobitism, Nicholas Rogers of popular Jacobitism in the early Hanoverian period and the present writer on Jacobite Parliamentary politics in the last years of Queen Anne, which appeared in the late 1970s and early 1980s, created some middle ground between the two schools of historiography but did not reconcile them, thus leaving ample room for future debate.[17]

The rejectionists

Even in the eighteenth century there was always a school of pro-establishment thought that found it difficult to believe that any but the most stupid or most desperate individuals would actively support the exiled dynasty.[18] Indeed, some Jacobites, such as the Earl of Barrymore, made very effective use of this prejudice to cover their tracks.[19] From this incomprehension of Jacobite motives in part stemmed the great Whig, progressivist tradition of historiography in which England, and subsequently the other kingdoms of the British Isles steadily, nigh inexorably progressed towards the constitutional, Parliamentary democracy of the present day. Lord Macaulay's sketch of what he believed the stereotypical Tory-Jacobite squire to have been like – a bigoted, ignorant, drunken philistine – is a telling example of the impatience of the Whig tradition with anti-progressive forces, as well as one of the most brilliantly devastating pieces of fiction ever produced by this school of thought.[20] For historians of this ilk throughout the nineteenth century, down to G. M. Trevelyan in the twentieth, Jacobitism could only ever occupy the margins of history.[21] It was defeated; *ergo* it could not have won. And of, course, there was little point in studying a seditious movement whose ethos was embedded in pre-industrial paternalism and mystical loyalism when these had both been supplanted by the sturdy individualism and rational self-interest the nineteenth-century Whig historians prized so highly.

Nor was the Whig tradition alone in taking this view of Jacobitism. Sir Lewis Namier, the doyen of the Tory/cynical school of interpretation, had just as little time for the Jacobite cause. In dealing with the demoralised rump of the Tory party in his microscopic studies of the structure of politics at the accession of George III, Namier found no evidence of serious Jacobitism amongst them and implicitly dismissed the phenomenon as a harmless affectation.[22] And where the greatest British historians have led, many others, scarcely lesser in stature, have followed. John Owen's unsurpassable study of the rise of the Pelhams 1742–6 contains barely a mention of Jacobites, Jacobitism or the '45 except insofar as they formed the backdrop for the Pelham brothers' manoeuvrings to rid themselves of their execrable rival Earl Granville.[23] Paul Langford's seminal work on the propertied classes of eighteenth-century England by and large ignores Jacobitism.[24] William Speck's entire *œuvre* finds it all rather irrelevant.[25] And Linda Colley's vigorous rehabilitation of the Tory party explicitly seeks to rebut Whig canards that it was Jacobite to the core.[26]

Jacobitism and the shape of British history

At the heart of these disputes about Jacobitism's prospects of success and its relevance or irrelevance to understanding eighteenth-century Britain lies a fundamental interpretative problem. If Jacobitism was not marginal to the mainstream of Britain's political development – as the interpretation embedded in most school textbooks would suggest – then the historical profession in Britain has got a lot of rethinking and reinterpretation of eighteenth and nineteenth century British history to do. As Jonathan Clark has provocatively suggested, if we accept that Jacobitism was a force to be reckoned with at all levels of the British polity, then we can find a continuous, deep vein of social and political conservatism running throughout British history at least up to the late 1820s.[27] This would radically alter our whole historical perspective on the last four centuries. The Great Civil War becomes little more than a belated attempt to stop an innovating king – something with which a great many medieval barons would have felt a good deal of sympathy. The Glorious Revolution, because it went against the grain of this conservatism, likewise becomes a Whig *coup d'état* with very shaky foundations, and so on. By this interpretation, Britain, rather than leading the world in the attainment of constitutional government and political stability (the conventional view), came to it very late. Maybe as late as the 1830s. If this argument can be sustained then many other classic interpretations fall to the ground. For example, Britain's legendary political stability cannot have helped precipitate the industrial revolution, as is assumed by so many economic historians, if it was not in fact stable, but

rather volatile. Likewise, if the dream of liberty kept alive by the
seamless vein of hidden political radicalism which historians like
Christopher Hill have detected coursing from the 1640s to the
1790s becomes instead the touchstone for a movement which to
twentieth-century eyes looks like the polar opposite of political
radicalism – Jacobitism – then what are we to make of working-
class agitation in the early nineteenth century? The dialectic of
history, in particular the gathering class consciousness of the
workers, is broken.[28]

The implications for the shape of British history are, then,
momentous if Jacobitism was central rather than peripheral in
the development of the British polity in the eighteenth century.
The first appearance of such a suggestion has therefore drawn
some heavy fire from those historians who believe it currently
enjoys its rightful, marginal place in our historiography. None
more wittily and bitterly than David Cannadine in his farewell
address to British academe in 1986. According to him, there
were four great heresies enervating British history in the 1980s:
myopic archive-grubbing, snobbish adulation of the aristocracy
and its way of life, politically inspired celebration of Thatcherite
individualism and:

> the new Jacobite view of history, a wilfully perverse celebration of
> such obscurantist troglodytes as the Young Pretender, the Tractarians
> and the Duke of Windsor, which makes even the embittered splutter-
> ings of Hilaire Belloc seem models of fair-mindedness and tolerance
> by comparison.[29]

This was not the end of the debate. It took on new strength
during the historical reflections that accompanied the tercentenary
of 1688, and as the body of serious historical analysis of the Jacobite
phenomenon grows it will intensify and spread.[30]

So how can a student newly arrived at the subject make a
reasonably informed judgement on how seriously she or he should
treat it? In the end there are no shortcuts. The present author
is part of the debate and cannot offer anything but a partisan
assessment. Hence the student who wants to move beyond the
introduction to Jacobitism offered below must read widely in
eighteenth-century British (*not* just English) history and make his or
her own assessment. But as a final surrender to my own prejudices
on the subject I invite every student who comes to the subject of

Jacobitism to indulge in a brief exercise in counterfactualism – or as Jonathan Clark pungently puts it, 'guessing'.

What if the infant James Francis Edward Stuart had died in the summer of 1688? He was a sickly child in his early infancy, largely, one feels, as a consequence of his anxious parents (who had lost a number of children in infancy by that time) giving in to the doctors' suggestion that he be fed on gruel laced with Canary wine and other quack remedies rather than breast milk, so it was perfectly possible that he might have expired before their idiocy was rectified.[31] If we then contemplate what might have changed if that one little infant had died, like so many of his late seventeenth-century peers, but everything else followed its natural course, we may be able to glimpse how much of a difference the Jacobites made to the course of British history.

For a start, it seems highly unlikely there would have been a revolution in the autumn of 1688, as the 'Immortal Seven' who invited William of Orange were only finally brought round to doing so by the ghastly prospect of a Roman Catholic male heir. No revolution then, or at least not one as sweeping and important as the Glorious Revolution. When James died in 1701 Princess Anne, his sole surviving and *Protestant* daughter (Princess Mary died in 1694) would have inherited the throne, on schedule for the War of Spanish Succession. Since Princess Louisa, James II and Mary of Modena's last child (born 1692) died of smallpox in 1712, there would still have been a succession crisis in 1714 when Queen Anne died without direct heirs. And since most of the nearer claimants were French Catholics, in all probability the reliably Protestant Hanoverians would still have inherited the three thrones of the British Isles. The net result then, of removing that infant in 1688 would probably have been to have secured the peaceful, uncontested succession of the Hanoverian dynasty. Thus the crises that punctuate the history of the period 1714–60 would in all likelihood never have occurred. There would have been no '15, no '45, no preparations for foreign invasions based on the premise of a Jacobite rebellion to support them, no Jacobite menace with which to keep angry Whig MPs in line, no threat of a disputed succession to impel English politicians to bribe, cajole and bully the reluctant Scots into a political union, no higher justification for the bridling of the Church of England. How different, and yet how uncannily familiar, the eighteenth-century British Isles would have been.

Notes

1 For examples of which see: P. Hopkins, *Glencoe and the End of the Highland War*, Edinburgh, 1986; P. Langford, *Public Life and the Propertied Englishman 1689–1798*, 1991; F. J. McLynn, *Charles Edward Stuart. A Tragedy in Many Acts*, 1988; E. Cruickshanks, *Political Untouchables. The Tories and the '45*, 1979.

2 J. Black, *British Foreign Policy in the Age of Walpole*, Edinburgh, 1985; G. S. Holmes, *British Politics in the Age of Anne*, 2nd edn, 1987; J. H. Plumb, *The Growth of Political Stability in England 1675–1725*, repr. 1977.

3 A debate which offers profound insights too into the way historical discourse edits the past, for which see A. J. Youngson's intriguing book, *The Prince and the Pretender. A Study in the Writing of History*, 1985.

4 For which see: C. Lamont, ed., Sir Walter Scott, *Waverley; or, 'Tis Sixty Years Since*, Oxford, 1981, and any of the rest of Scott's Jacobite novels, culminating in *Redgauntlet*. The 'optimist' school, however, may be missing Scott's hidden agenda, for, as, Murray Pittock has pointed out, all his Jacobite characters are either anachronisms or dangerous children. M. G. H. Pittock, *The Invention of Scotland. The Stuart Myth and the Scottish Identity, 1638 to the Present*, 1991, p. 34.

5 For examples of Hanoverian black propaganda, see: R. C. Jarvis, *Collected Papers on the Jacobite Risings*, 2 vols. Manchester, 1972, II, pp. 122–37, 189–201, 208–9; for the domestication of Jacobitism see, Pittock, *Invention of Scotland*, pp. 99–105.

6 For examples of which see: W. D. Macray, ed., *Correspondence of Colonel N. Hooke, Agent From the Court of France to the Scottish Jacobites, in the Years 1703–7*, 2 vols., Roxburghe Club, 1870; E. Buckley, ed., *Memoirs of Thomas, Earl of Ailesbury. Written by Himself*, 2 vols., Roxburghe Club, 1890; E. Charteris, ed., *A Short Account of the Affairs of Scotland in the Years 1744, 1745, 1746. By David Lord Elcho*, Edinburgh, 1907; A. and H. Tayler, *Jacobites of Aberdeenshire and Banffshire*, 1928; *Jacobite Letters to Lord Pitsligo*, 1930.

7 *The Jacobite Movement*, 1st edn, 1932; *The Marshal Duke of Berwick*, 1953; 'The Elibank plot, 1752–3', *Transactions of the Royal Historical Society*, XIV, 1931, pp. 175–6; 'The Jacobite activities in south and west England in summer 1715', *Transactions of the Royal Historical Society*, II, 1935, pp. 85–106.

8 Petrie, *Jacobite Movement*, 1st edn, appendix VI: 'A Jacobite fantasy', pp. 300–5.

9 R. Sedgwick, ed., *The House of Commons 1715–54*, 2 vols., 1970, I, pp. 62–78.

10 *Political Untouchables, passim.*

11 *France and the Jacobite Rising of 1745*, Edinburgh, 1981.

12 *Glencoe, passim.*

13 *Jacobitism and the English People, 1688–1788*, 1989.

14 *The Main Stream of Jacobitism*, Cambridge, Massachusetts, 1954.

15 'Was Queen Anne a Jacobite?', *History*, LVII, 1972, pp. 358–75; *Queen Anne*, 1980.

16 P. S. Fritz, *The English Ministers and Jacobitism Between the Rebellions of 1715 and 1745*, 1975; G. V. Bennett, *The Tory Crisis in Church and State, 1688–1730. The Career of Francis Atterbury, Bishop of Rochester*, 1975.

17 B. Lenman, *The Jacobite Risings in Britain 1689–1746*, 1980; N. Rogers, 'Popular disaffection in London during the Forty-Five', *The London Journal*, I, 1975, pp. 5–27; 'Resistance to oligarchy: the City opposition to Walpole and his successors, 1725–47', in, J. Stevenson, ed., *London in the Age of Reform*, Oxford, 1977; 'Popular protest in early Hanoverian London', *Past and Present*, LXXIX, 1978, pp. 70–100; D. Szechi, *Jacobitism and Tory Politics 1710–14*, Edinburgh, 1984.

18 R. Sedgwick, ed., *Some Materials Towards Memoirs of the Reign of King George II, By John, Lord Hervey*, 3 vols, 1931, I, pp. 4–6.

19 Sedgwick, *House of Commons*, I, pp. 440–2.

20 T. B. Macaulay, *The History of England From the Accession of James the Second*, ed. C. Firth, 6 vols, New York, repr. 1968, I, pp. 310–13.

21 G. M. Trevelyan, *England Under Queen Anne: Blenheim*, repr. 1935, pp. 151–2, 158, 161, 174, 327; *England Under Queen Anne. The Peace and the Protestant Succession*, repr. 1948, pp. 89–90, 310–19.

22 L. Namier, *The Structure of Politics at the Accession of George III*, repr. 2nd edn, 1982; *England in the Age of the American Revolution*, repr. 2nd edn, 1970, p. 183.

23 *The Rise of the Pelhams*, 1957.

24 *Public Life; A Polite and Commercial People. England 1727–1783*, Oxford, 1989.

25 *Tory and Whig. The Struggle in the Constituencies*, 1970; 'Whigs and Tories dim their glories', in J. Cannon, ed., *The Whig Ascendancy. Colloquies on Hanoverian England*, 1981. Cf. *The Butcher. The Duke of Cumberland and the Suppression of the '45*, 1981.

26 *In Defiance of Oligarchy. The Tory Party 1714–60*, 1982.

27 *Revolution and Rebellion. State and Society in England in the Seventeenth and Eighteenth Centuries*, 1986; and especially, 'On moving the middle ground: the significance of Jacobitism in historical studies', in E. Cruickshanks and J. Black, eds., *The Jacobite Challenge*, Edinburgh, 1988, pp. 177–85.

28 Clark, 'Moving the middle ground', pp. 178–9.

29 'The state of British history', *Times Literary Supplement*, 10 October 1986, p. 1140.

30 R. Beddard, 'The unexpected Whig revolution of 1688', in R. Beddard, ed., *The Revolutions of 1688. The Andrew Browning Lectures*

Introduction

1988, Oxford, 1991, pp. 11–101; W. A. Speck, *Reluctant Revolutionaries. Englishmen and the Revolution of 1688*, 1988; D. Szechi, 'Mythistory versus history: the fading of the Revolution of 1688', *Historical Journal*, XXXIII, 1990, pp. 143–53.

31 J. Miller, *James II. A Study in Kingship*, Hove, 1977, pp. 186–7.

11

1

Jacobite society

In 1932 Sir Charles Petrie described Jacobitism as a 'definite political movement',[1] manifestly intending to evoke comparison with such twentieth-century phenomena as the Labour movement or the Workers' Educational Association. In principle he was being anachronistic, but as is often the case with such analogies he was closer in spirit to a crucial aspect of the Jacobite experience than perhaps even he realised. Anyone who has participated in a modern political movement can testify that although they may initially have joined the party (or the organisation) for entirely principled, rational reasons, their commitment soon begins to shade over into their social life. As time goes on, more and more of their friends and acquaintances will be connected with the movement, and more and more of their leisure time will reflect their involvement, even if only to the extent of reading a 'politically correct' newspaper or patronising businesses that 'do the right thing'. Jacobitism was not a modern political movement, but like twentieth-century movements it was associated with a distinct social milieu.

In abstract terms, Jacobitism generated an introverted commensality within British society, i.e. it produced a self-sustaining, recognisable minority who rejected the social, political and religious order installed after 1688. Clustered around this nucleus was a shifting cloud of individuals, families and connexions (kinship and friendship networks focused on an individual or a family) who were drawn into opposition to the established order for various reasons, but were never as resolutely committed as the core group. The nucleus's sub-culture was the heart of the Jacobite cause in

Britain and it was able to survive for as long as it did only because of the peculiarities of eighteenth-century British society. Before taking a closer look at Jacobite society in Britain then, we must first briefly review how British society as a whole functioned.

Hierarchy and power in Britain, 1688–1788

Eighteenth-century English (and Welsh) society conceived of itself as a hierarchy of orders.[2] Men and women were born into a certain station in life – yeoman, gentleman, artisan, etc. – and moved up or down the social hierarchy within that compartment for the rest of their days. Some of course completely lost their place in the order due to personal or impersonal disasters, and plummeted down into the dreaded category of the rootless, hopeless, vagrant poor. Still other exceptional individuals would make a dramatic success of their lives and ascend into a higher order, where they would always be regarded with suspicion as *nouveaux riches*, but their grandchildren would be accepted and the family subsumed by their new rank. Each order of society was supposed to look to those above it for cultural, moral and political leadership, and atop the pyramid sat a tiny elite of landowner-aristocrats who were its natural rulers. It was a society that was hostile to social mobility (except at the lowest levels) and in which lines of authority were apparently clear-cut: only one person in England had no human master, and that was the monarch.

Theory and actuality are often very different things, and this was certainly the case in eighteenth-century England. The period 1660–1832 was one in which a new perception of the social order was steadily hammering its way like a battering-ram through the traditional facade of caste and hierarchy.[3] Novel ties of authority and allegiance were overlaying the custom of former generations, distorting them and edging them out. Well-to-do bourgeois, and especially the burgeoning manufacturer group among them, were increasingly (though as yet spasmodically) uniting in pursuit of an economic, social and political agenda that addressed their common concerns. Meanwhile their apprentices and servants more and more found themselves treated in a way previously reserved for the itinerant poor: they were paid for their labour but otherwise left to their own devices. Fewer and fewer masters were concerned with the physical and spiritual welfare of their men. Divergent religious beliefs, sheltered by the grudging religious toleration conceded to Protestant Dissenters in 1689, sapped the vitality of the traditional order too. Because England's rulers had traditionally taken religious uniformity to be a vital component in the maintenance of social stability and public acceptance of the authority of the powers-that-were, the mere existence of Protestant religious nonconformity implicitly challenged the authority of the English *ancien régime*.

Despite the pervasiveness of these developments English society changed only slowly. At least 80 per cent of the population lived in old communities, primarily small market towns and rural hamlets, in which the power and authority of squire, master and parson remained basically intact throughout the eighteenth century. In the handful of English cities with more than 10,000 population, such as London, Bristol and Norwich, the decay of the old order was more rapid and visible, but they too preserved the rudiments of the *ancien régime* at least as late as the 1790s.

The most convincing analysis so far developed of the basic dynamics of relations between rulers and ruled in this changing, creaking, riven society is that of E. P. Thompson, who divided eighteenth-century English society into two theoretical groupings: 'patricians' and 'plebeians'.[4] 'Patricians' basically subsumes all those who ruled: wealthy London merchants, hard-faced Birmingham ironmasters, penurious aristocrats, comfortable landed gentry, and so on. 'Plebeians' subsumes those who were ruled: small shopkeepers and traders; journeymen; apprentices; day labourers; thieves and whores, etc. Relations between these two groups were arbitrated by a 'moral economy' in which the rich had a duty to ensure the poor could secure at least a minimal subsistence and the poor had a duty to be respectful and obey their betters. The unspoken understanding was that if the patricians did not do their duty the poor would do it for them – by rioting and thereby appropriating the necessities of life.[5] The moral economy, moreover, was not restricted solely to achieving bread-and-butter objectives. A persistent feature of its operations was the preservation of the customs of the small rural and urban communities where it operated most effectively. Thus uppity Nonconformists or Catholics, swaggering Whig bravos or pickpockets and prostitutes released by corrupt or inefficient magistrates were as likely to find themselves the targets of violent popular disapproval as engrossing grain merchants or short-changing shopkeepers.[6] There was almost no aspect of English life outside the purview of the moral economy.

Except in the Highlands, Scottish society in many ways reflected the impact of the same developments that were transforming England and Wales. In the lowlands of southern Scotland and the valleys of the north-east the social hierarchy was very similar to that in England, and correspondingly the market-driven forces of social and cultural change affected them in like fashion. The main difference was that the power of the market, and thus the force powering change, was weaker in Scotland. Something in the region of 90 per cent of Scotland's population derived their livelihood from the land for most of the eighteenth century. Until the development of economic magnets like Glasgow in the mid- to late eighteenth century the transformation of Scottish society could thus proceed only slowly. The authority of the old order was seriously compromised in certain areas by competing religious ties, so that Cameronian preachers could overrule the *dictat* of the laird in parts of the south-east and Episcopalian ministers defy the authority of local presbyteries in parts of the north-east,[7] but overall the accustomed rulers of society continued to reign in much the same manner as their forebears.

Scottish Highland society was distinctively different for most of the Jacobite period. Gaelic-speaking and poor, the clans eking out a living in the Highlands and islands preserved a unique social organisation designed to sustain them through the chronic vicissitudes of their harsh environment.[8] Each clan had a ruling dynasty with an associated mythology. The dynasty and its cadet branches provided the hereditary rulers of the clan in peace and war, while the mythology provided the focus for clan unity by promoting belief in the descent of all members of the clan from a common ancestor and hence participation in various epic events. More than anything else, the feature of clan society that made it unique in the British Isles by the eighteenth century was that it was a society geared for war. The most important obligation the junior officers of the clan's ruling dynasty, the Tacksmen, owed the chieftain was the manrent, i.e. the quota of armed men they were required to provide and lead in the clan's cause. This meant that Highland chieftains could mobilise private armies whenever they judged it opportune. They were not absolute rulers, for they had to carry the Tacksmen with them, and the Tacksmen in turn had to persuade the rank-and-file clansmen to follow them and the chieftain, but by and large the chieftains usually got their way. And because of the general belief in the intertwining fortunes of clan and dynasty, the chieftain's authority in all other spheres of life usually went unchallenged. Change in such a society could only come from the top. Thus the ordinary clansmen saw little benefit from the integration of the Highlands into the national economy in the late seventeenth century – the clan elite took all the surpluses that accrued from it. The clan elites were, though, not unaffected by the wider changes affecting Scottish society, which they were exposed to while they busily dissipated whatever surpluses the Highland economy provided in Paris, Edinburgh and London. The relatively untrammelled authority they enjoyed in the Highlands meant, however, they were generally able to contain the impact of these changes on clan society until the mid-eighteenth century.

By the early eighteenth century the last remnants of the old pastoral Irish economy had withered away, to be replaced by conventional arable agriculture on the English model. And on the surface an English pattern of social relations prevailed too. Recent research has shown that for most of the time a moral economy operated in Ireland along the same lines as in England and Wales.[9] What was of course different was the religious complexion of the various strata of Irish society. Throughout Ireland, with the sole exception of parts of Ulster, the plebeians were overwhelmingly Catholic. In those parts of Ulster most heavily settled by seventeenth-century Scots colonists they were mainly Presbyterian Nonconformists. Everywhere in the kingdom almost all the patricians were Church of Ireland (Anglican) Protestants. Because the religious complexion of Irish society reflected, in the main, the disposition of privilege and power, the moral economy was thus very much more limited in its 'legitimate' operation in Ireland than in England. There can be no question, for example, that the authority of the local Catholic clergy and their Presbyterian counterparts normally outweighed that of the local patricians if the two came into conflict.[10] In addition, the ancient division between the 'Old Irish', who were still mainly Gaelic-speakers and descended from the original occupants of the island, and the 'Old English', who were English-speakers descended from its medieval Anglo-Norman conquerers, continued to divide the

Catholics and complicate the exercise of patrician authority well into the eighteenth century.[11]

The structure of Jacobite society

Jacobite society had three discernible layers. Its inner kernel consisted of the hard-core, ideologically committed Jacobites; men and women who stood aloof as far as they were able from post-Revolutionary society and brought up their children to follow the true path after them. Around this inner group there was always a thicker layer of the politically embittered. These were individuals or connexions who were not congenitally averse to operating in the post-Revolutionary world, but had become disillusioned or disgruntled or simply lost out in the political game and were seeking a radical way to re-enter the fray. This layer of Jacobites tended to drift into and out of association with active Jacobitism depending on its political fortunes and the likelihood of a Jacobite restoration. If the Jacobites seemed to have a serious prospect of success support from this layer was likely to be firm; conversely, when the cause was in the doldrums it tended to lose interest. The final, outer layer of the Jacobite commensality was very thin, indeed it could only ever be a small percentage of the whole group: the adventurers. These were the least reliable part of Jacobite society, the desperate men driven to Jacobitism for lack of any other means of mending their fortunes. Bankrupts, wastrels and the irredeemably politically disgraced, they had little or nothing to lose and everything to gain if the Jacobites won, which guaranteed their enthusiasm for the cause when it was in the ascendant. Conversely, they had little or no compunction about abandoning or betraying it when it no longer offered them any prospect of worldly success. All of these groups played a vital role in Jacobite society which needs to be separately explored, and the characteristics of each can best be introduced by considering the kind of man who typifies that layer of Jacobitism's adherents.

Thomas Syddall was a classic example of mid-eighteenth-century social mobility. His father was a blacksmith in Manchester, but Thomas junior took up the trade of wigmaker, and by specialising in the field of luxury perukes made a fortune estimated at £2,000 by the time of his death in 1746. Thomas's father was one of the ringleaders of a series of Jacobite riots that convulsed Manchester

17

early in 1715, and was subsequently executed for joining the rebellion later the same year. Thomas himself became a devout member of the strict Nonjuring church led by Thomas Deacon in Manchester, and was a friend of Deacon's sons and the Jacobite poet John Byrom.[12] When Charles Edward Stuart's army entered Manchester in the course of its foray into England Syddall immediately enlisted, and as befitted a municipal patrician, was made an officer of the newly formed Manchester regiment. Captured at Carlisle with the rest of the regiment, he was tried and executed for his part in the rebellion, but died defiant, exhorting his fellow-countrymen:

> in the name of God, to restore your liege sovereign, and with him the glorious advantages of an excellent constitution under a lawful government. This is every man's duty to aim at: and if your honest attempts should fail, remember, it is a great blessing to die for the cause of virtue; and that an almighty power can, and will, reward such as suffer for righteousness sake.[13]

The bedrock of Jacobitism in Britain, as exemplified by Syddall, lay in the congregations of three churches: the Roman Catholic, the Anglican Nonjuring and the Scots Episcopalian. The Catholics were a tiny minority in England and Scotland (c.2 per cent in England and c.1 per cent in Scotland) and the majority (c.75 per cent) of the population of Ireland. The Irish Catholic community (especially the Gaelic-speaking Old Irish) was also steadily becoming more and more plebeian as the patrician Catholic element faded away under the pressure of the penal laws. In the Highlands a few Catholic clans, like the Macdonalds of Clanranald, survived into the eighteenth century, but they were exceptions to the progressive decapitation of the Catholic community elsewhere in the Gaelic-speaking British Isles. Conversely in England and lowland Scotland the Catholic community was dominated by the surviving Catholic gentry, and the few plebeian Catholics who were not of Irish descent tended to be their tenants or servants.[14] Accustomed as it was, however, to subterfuge and secrecy by nearly 200 years of official repression, the Catholic church and its adherents in Britain were uniquely well equipped to support the Jacobite cause and enthusiastically did so in every major Jacobite rebellion. Thus they were always a disproportionately large element in Jacobite armies as well as assiduous contributors to the financial upkeep of the Jacobite court. An attempt in the late 1710s by an 'accommodationist' group of clergy and laity, headed by the Duke of Norfolk, formally to reconcile themselves with the Hanoverian regime by taking suitably adjusted oaths to the dynasty was scotched by vigorous internal opposition within the Catholic community,[15] and thereafter the question of anything more than tactical compromises with the existing order never arose. As a result, by the 1770s, when almost everyone else had effectively deserted the exiled Stuarts, many of them still faithfully clung to the dynasty.[16]

The Nonjurors were based on a group of about 400 Anglican clergy who refused to take new oaths of allegiance[17] to William and Mary while James II still lived. Initially the Nonjurors were not a church but a devout, intellectual coterie of divines supported and sheltered by a handful of lay patrons. A small group among them, however, led by Francis Turner, the former Bishop of Ely, and George Hickes, decided to perpetuate their schism with the Church of England by ordaining new clergymen for the Nonjuror community in the mid-1690s when they realised that James II was not likely soon to be restored.[18] From this decision a fully schismatic Anglican church arose in the early 1700s which drew to itself small but stiff-necked congregations in all the major English cities and a scattering of patrician country houses. There were never very many Nonjurors – one recent estimate puts them at about 1 per cent of the patrician elite – but they were dedicated Jacobites. Because they remained visibly Protestant too, they were better situated actively to agitate for the Jacobite cause, and thus they too were to be found in disproportionate numbers in every Jacobite riot and rebellion. Relative to their numbers they consequently also provided more martyrs for the cause than any other group.[19]

Catholics and Nonjurors both contributed large contingents to Jacobite armies, but the bulk of the rank-and-file always came from the Scots Episcopalians. Without them the Jacobite cause would have been a feeble thing indeed, yet in some ways they form a 'halfway house' between the ideologically committed Catholics and Nonjurors and the more volatile groups of disgruntled politicians intermittently associated with the Jacobite cause. In part this may be because there were so many of them. At a guess, there may have been as many as 200,000 Catholics and Nonjurors in mainland

Britain. Without a doubt there were at least 200,000 Scots Episcopalians. Primarily located in the Highlands and the north-eastern lowlands north of the river Tay, from the early 1690s onwards they constituted a semi-alienated community, allowed (as Protestants) to take part in Scottish politics, but permanently in a minority, and periodically subjected to discriminatory legislation by the Presbyterian establishment in Kirk and State.[20] Many if not most patrician Episcopalians were sympathetic to the Jacobite cause, and because of their greater authority over the Scottish plebeians on their estates, whole areas followed their lead. As a consequence of their semi-legal status, however, there was always a significant 'accommodationist' tendency within the Episcopalian community, which expressed itself in clergymen like James Greenshields and John Paterson, Archbishop of Glasgow, and politicians like the 4th Duke of Hamilton.[21] This tendency was either silent on the subject of the exiled dynasty, or at most paid it lip-service; their aim was to get along with the powers-that-were. After the crushing defeat the activists took in 1746, the collaborationist tendency moved to the fore, and from 1760 onwards the Scots Episcopalian church and its adherents enjoyed steadily improving relations with the Hanoverian regime. When Charles 'III' died in 1788 the Episcopalians finally abandoned the Stuarts and, apart from eccentric hold-outs like the Oliphants of Gask, were completely reconciled to the new (by then rather ripe) order.

John Erskine, 11th Earl of Mar, typifies the kind of disgruntled politician who sometimes ended up associated with the Jacobite cause in the first half of the eighteenth century. Though he stemmed from an Episcopalian background he never let this impair his ambition. Early in his career he aligned himself with the careerist, Scottish 'Revolution interest' headed by the Duke of Queensberry. By the time of the Union in 1707 he was well established as a minor power in Scottish politics, having worked his way up as Queensberry's lieutenant. Amply rewarded by Queen Anne for his part in steering the Act of Union through the Scottish Parliament, he settled quickly into British politics, where he deftly outmanoeuvred all his rivals to make himself the Harley ministry's key man of business for Scotland by 1711. The pinnacle of his career in conventional politics came in 1713 when the post of Secretary of State for Scotland was specifically revived for him, shortly followed by his successful negotiation of a lucrative marriage with the daughter of the wealthy Whig Earl of Kingston.

Unfortunately for Mar, in the process of rising so high so fast he had become inextricably associated with the Harley ministry in the mind of the incoming dynasty. Thus, despite his best efforts to ingratiate himself with it after Queen Anne's death, he found himself purged from office in favour of a rival magnate, the Whig Duke of Montrose. Burdened with heavy debts, and fearing his Scottish Whig enemies would impeach him for his part in the ministry that had negotiated that Hanoverian and Whig *bête noire*, the Peace of Utrecht of 1713, Mar despairingly turned to Jacobitism. Though he was a clever and effective politician, he was at best a mediocre general, and the failure of the '15 stemmed in large part from his incompetence. Fleeing Scotland in company with his putative king, Mar was appointed James's Secretary of State and ran the Jacobite underground for three years (1716–19). By this time, however, he had become embittered and abrasive and was in the end forced to resign and go into retirement. From there in 1721–2 he tried to work his passage home by betraying the inner workings of the Atterbury plot to the British government. The plot was duly foiled, but he was denied his reward. He finally died, shunned, friendless and still in exile, in 1732.[22]

If the three churches most decisively alienated by the Revolution provided the bedrock of the Jacobite cause, the political alignments that lost out during the Revolution Settlement and after constituted its hope of salvation. The prospect of large-scale support for the exiled Stuarts from beyond the charmed circle of Jacobitism's traditional constituency was a potent lure for foreign powers, who wanted the maximum possible reassurance that their invading armies would not find themselves abandoned and isolated in the English countryside. Consequently from 1692 onwards the Jacobite court did its best to woo politically disaffected groups in British politics. Nor were these groups indifferent to the glittering prizes a Jacobite restoration might offer to those who engineered it. In the 1690s a number of Whigs who were dissatisfied with the Revolution Settlement's moderation, or resented their treatment by William III, accordingly opened negotiations with Jacobite agents. Most, like Admiral Russell and the Duke of Shrewsbury in 1692, were soon revealed merely to have been engaging in reinsurance in case a Jacobite restoration occurred despite them. But a few, such as Sir James Montgomerie of Skelmorlie, Robert Ferguson and Charlwood Lawton, seem to have undergone a genuine conversion.[23] Overall, however, there can be no doubt that very few Whigs ever seriously considered the Jacobite option, though the Jacobites patiently sounded out every dissident Whig group from the 1690s to the 1730s in the hope of finding allies amongst them.[24] The only exception to this was in Scotland, where Whiggish Scots patriots like the 10th Earl Marischal and the Master of Sinclair were left nowhere else to go than Jacobitism after 1707 if they wished to free Scotland from English domination. Likewise, for a short time before and after the Union (1706–8), hard-line Presbyterian patriots, like the Cameronians, who could normally be safely regarded as rock-solid supporters of all that was anti-Jacobite, turned briefly to Jacobitism in the hope of restoring Scotland's liberties.[25]

The prize the Jacobite court sought most earnestly from the late 1690s onwards was the Tory party. The Tories were the heirs of the old Cavaliers, who had stuck with Charles II through the Exclusion Crisis and offered, albeit unenthusiastically, to support James II in 1688. Furthermore, their formal political ideology centred on loyalty to the Church of England and loyalty to the monarchy. The problem for the Jacobites was that post-Revolutionary Tories' core beliefs had precisely that order of priorities: church first, monarchy second.[26] And since most Tories did not believe the church could ever be safe under a Catholic dynasty, this put them beyond the Jacobites' reach for most of the period 1688–1788. Nonetheless, intermittently, when large numbers of Tories feared for the safety of the church or felt particularly aggrieved with the government, an alliance that embraced many, if not most, Tories, would coalesce. This happened in 1715–22 and 1743–5, on the first occasion because the Hanoverian regime appeared to be dismantling the Anglican dominance in church and state, and on the second because the Tories had just been betrayed by their dissident Whig allies, and hence on the very threshold of power (the 'Country' alliance had finally succeeded in bringing down Sir Robert Walpole) denied the fruits of a victory they believed to be rightfully theirs.[27] The Tories were basically fainthearts whenever serious action was in prospect, but there was always the chance that a foreign power impressed by their transient zeal might invade, and even draw large numbers of the Tories into turning out to fight – if it looked like winning.

The third layer of Jacobitism was composed of adventurers – the desperate men of eighteenth-century British society. William Boyd, 4th Earl of Kilmarnock, is an almost archetypal example of the breed.[28] Scion of an old Cavalier family reduced to straitened circumstances by improvidence after the Restoration, he inherited estates so heavily mortgaged that all he could look forward to was a future of, at best, genteel poverty. His only lifeline, a government pension, was cut off by Lord Wilmington in the aftermath of Walpole's fall, and he was reduced to 'plaguing' his estate steward (by the 1740s virtually an employee of Kilmarnock's creditors) for sums of a few shillings at a time. The Jacobite rebellion consequently appeared to him as a heaven-sent opportunity, and urged on by his ardently Catholic and Jacobite wife he joined Charles Edward after the battle of Prestonpans, though, as he admitted to the Duke of Argyll later:

> for the two Kings and their rights, I cared not a farthing which prevailed; but I was starving, and, by God, if Mahommed had set up his standard in the Highlands I had been a good Mussulman for bread, and stuck close to the party, for I must eat.[29]

Charles welcomed and rewarded him, making him a colonel and privy counsellor and, after a brave performance at the battle of Falkirk, even promoting him to the rank of general. Poor Kilmarnock was, however, captured while still fighting hard for the Jacobite cause at the battle of Culloden, and though he tried to work his passage with the government, was duly executed as a warning to other men of desperate fortunes of the fate that awaited them.

Jacobite adventurers came from all walks of life. They ranged from patrician ex-army officers down on their luck to unemployed plebeian weavers looking for excitement.[30] There was always a smattering of them involved in any Jacobite activity, and, more perniciously, they provided the main recruiting ground for spies and informers. The reasons for this are obvious: they had no deep commitment to the cause, and if it could not provide them with financial sustenance they had few scruples about selling what they knew to anyone who would pay. There were never very many adventurers associated with the Jacobite cause, but they did fulfil a vital role. They acted as a leaven. The Catholics,

Nonjurors and Episcopalians gave the cause its backbone; the politically disaffected gave it foreign and domestic credibility; the adventurers gave Jacobitism its dynamism. Without rascals like Coll Macdonald of Keppoch, John Campbell of Glenorchy (1st Earl of Breadalbane), John Murray of Broughton and their English and Irish counterparts, the Jacobites' conduct would have been far less daring, and it is doubtful if they would ever have seriously threatened the stability of the British state.[31] The adventurers overcame the intelligent, prudent caution that might otherwise have overwhelmed the movement.

The Jacobite milieu

Jacobite society in Britain revolved around networks of kinship and sociability. In some ways the other core groups within Jacobitism were simply emulating the endogamous, but widespread, family connexions the Anglo-Scottish Catholic community had used to preserve itself for the previous 200 years.[32] Endogamy ensured the next generation was brought up in the right political and religious principles, and that those steeped in the lore and beliefs of Jacobitism were not lost to the cause.[33] Marriage patterns dedicated to sustaining 'sound' family connections can, however, only really explain how patrician Jacobitism survived. Plebeians rarely married endogamously or even within the locality from which they originated. Their kith and kin changed from generation to generation, and yet certain wards in the major cities and areas in the countryside remained obstinately Jacobite from generation to generation. In the country this often stemmed from the abiding commitment to the cause of local landowners, though we should not underrate the ability of plebeian connexions to formulate and pass on their own perception of political reality. In the cities plebeian Jacobitism seems to have settled early in certain areas, and as like attracts like, generated its own semi-permanent sub-culture. In the case of areas like Shadwell which had a large Catholic Irish immigrant population its origins are self-evident, but in other areas of the same city, like Whitechapel, it seems to have been a precocious plebeian creation.[34]

Everywhere there were substantial numbers of Jacobites there were bound to be Jacobite alehouses, inns and taverns. Whether they were run by sympathetic landlords, or simply businessmen with an eye to the main chance, most plebeian Jacobites as a result had a 'social space' that was peculiarly their own. There they could fraternise with people of like mind, sing seditious songs, tell salacious stories about the Hanoverians, give money to sustain Jacobite prisoners, and even on occasion be recruited for Jacobite risings. And it is remarkable quite how often the kind of conviviality associated with hostelries like the Bull's Head in Manchester features in the careers of men who eventually became Jacobite rebels.[35] The government certainly believed these places to be nests of sedition, surreptitiously organised Whig 'Mughouse' gangs to attack well-known Jacobite haunts and occasionally closed down the more notorious of them, but to no avail: the customers would simply appropriate another venue and carry on as before. Patricians were not excluded from these nexuses of plebeian Jacobite sociability, but they were not so dependent on them for relaxation in the company of like-minded individuals because of their kinship connexions and the flourishing network of exclusively patrician Jacobite clubs that arose in early eighteenth-century Britain. The Cycle of the White Rose, the Sea Sergeants and numerous lodges of early Freemasons were all part of a wider network of patrician conviviality with an overtly Jacobite tinge.[36]

Stemming directly from the sociability and would-be exclusiveness of Jacobite society was a minor, subsidiary economy. In many ways this indirectly sustained the Jacobite social and religious milieu. Patrician Jacobites liked having pictures of the exiled royal family and of old Jacobite and Cavalier martyrs hanging on the walls of their homes. Accordingly a pool of Jacobite limners developed. Plebeian Jacobites were fond of singing rousing ballads that damned the Hanoverian regime and extolled the virtues of the Stuarts. Jacobite printers and ballad-hawkers soon cashed in on the demand for such wares. Jacobite knick-knacks: inscribed glassware, brooches with hidden symbols, tartan waistcoats, white roses on 10 June (the Old Pretender's birthday) and so on, all sold well in selected neighbourhoods. Minor industries duly appeared to serve this market.[37] There was a thriving market too for Jacobite pamphlets (and their rebuttals) and newspapers from the 1690s onwards. Jacobite journalists, writers and hacks, like Nathaniel Mist, Thomas Ruddiman and George Flint, promptly stepped forward to satisfy their public's appetite.[38] More dangerously, Jacobitism became involved with that peculiarly eighteenth-century

25

English version of organised crime: smuggling. English smugglers who professed to be (or actually were) Jacobites had an easy entrée into the merchant community of the French Atlantic seaboard, which was riddled with Jacobite exiles, and were thus able to ply their trade more freely. In England and Scotland sympathetic landowners aided and abetted smugglers for both political and economic reasons, thereby promoting some of the most difficult public-order problems British governments have ever had to deal with.[39] Taken broadly, the deep, diverse roots of all this anti-establishment economic and social activity created nothing short of an intractable problem for the eighteenth-century British state.

The kinship networks, economy and conviviality associated with British Jacobitism all help explain how Jacobitism survived, but ultimately they are merely symptoms of something deeper. In the final analysis it was Jacobitism's power to move men and women to personal sacrifice that sustained the cause for so long. And that came directly out of the religious commitment that tinged every aspect of the Jacobite milieu (see documents 2 and 6). The religious complexion of Jacobitism has already been described; the religious intensity derived from it touched all the confessional alignments that made it up. Essentially, from the exiled Stuart royal family downwards the term that best characterises Jacobite religious practice is *dévot*. Whether they were Catholic or Protestant, most of the men and women who were involved in Jacobitism were piously, deeply committed to their respective faiths. Indeed, it was through religious motifs that Nonjurors, Anglicans and Scots Episcopalians all shared, such as the doctrines of passive obedience, non-resistance and indefeasible hereditary right, that Jacobitism was able consistently to draw fresh recruits from among the more devout Tories (its best source of new blood).[40] The adventurers were obviously an exception to this pattern of commitment, but they were only ever a handful at any particular time. And wherever there was a significant Jacobite minority, or a landowning patrician Jacobite family, there was bound to be a chapel with a dissident clergyman, whether Catholic, Nonjuror, Episcopalian or Anglican crypto-Jacobite. These clergymen were the very soul of the Jacobite cause in Britain. They educated the children of Jacobite sympathisers in their classrooms and reinforced the message daily in their sermons.[41] Without them Jacobitism could never have survived as long as it did.

Notes

1 Petrie, *Jacobite Movement*, iii.

2 P. J. Corfield, 'Class by name and number in eighteenth-century Britain', *History*, LXXII, 1987, pp. 39–41.

3 Ibid., *passim*.

4 E. P. Thompson, *Customs in Common*, New York, 1991, pp. 16–96.

5 Ibid., pp. 185–258.

6 See for example: G. S. Holmes, *The Trial of Dr Sacheverell*, 1973, pp. 156–78; R. B. Shoemaker, 'The London 'mob' in the early eighteenth century', *Journal of British Studies*, XXVI, 1987, pp. 273–304.

7 Lenman, *Jacobite Risings*, pp. 57–67.

8 E. Richards, *A History of the Highland Clearances. Agrarian Transformation and the Evictions 1746–1886*, 1982, pp. 44–69.

9 T. Bartlett, 'An end to moral economy: the Irish militia disturbances of 1793', in C. H. E. Philpin, ed., *Nationalism and Popular Protest in Ireland*, 1987, pp. 192–3, 216–17.

10 T. W. Moody and W. E. Vaughan, eds., *A New History of Ireland. IV, Eighteenth-Century Ireland*, Oxford, 1986, pp. 38, 40–1.

11 Ibid., p. 53.

12 Monod, *Jacobitism*, pp. 241, 333.

13 *True Copies of the Dying Declarations of Arthur Lord Balmerino, Thomas Syddall, David Morgan, George Fletcher, John Berwick, Thomas Theodorus Deacon, Thomas Chadwick, James Dawson, Andrew Blyde, Donald Macdonald Esq, the Rev. Mr Thomas Coppoch, the Rev. Mr Robert Lyon, Edmund Clavering, John Hamilton Esq, James Bradshaw, Alexander Leith, and Andrew Wood*, Edinburgh, 1750, p. 13. See also the last speeches of Sir John Ashton and Archibald Cameron in the appendix of documents.

14 J. Bossy, *The English Catholic Community 1570–1850*, 1976, pp. 172–81.

15 J. C. D. Clark, ed., *The Memoirs and Speeches of James, 2nd Earl Waldegrave, 1742–63*, 1988, p. 23.

16 Monod, *Jacobitism*, pp. 137–8.

17 Hence the name, which comes from the Latin term for someone who refuses to take an oath.

18 *Dictionary of National Biography*, XXVI, p. 352.

19 Monod, *Jacobitism*, pp. 138–45, 270.

20 B. Lenman, 'The Scottish episcopal clergy and the ideology of Jacobitism', in E. Cruickshanks, ed., *Ideology and Conspiracy. Aspects of Jacobitism, 1689–1759*, Edinburgh, 1982, pp. 39–40.

21 HMC Portland MSS, X, pp. 379–81: Greenshields to the Earl of Oxford, 28 January and 27 August 1712; A. Aufrere, ed., *The Lockhart Papers*, 2 vols., 1817, I, pp. 84–5; P. W. J. Riley, *The Union of England and Scotland*, Manchester, 1978, pp. 268–70.

22 E. Gregg, 'The Jacobite career of John Earl of Mar', in Cruickshanks, *Ideology and Conspiracy*, pp. 179–200.

23 P. K. Monod, 'Jacobitism and Country principles in the reign of William III', *Historical Journal*, XXX, 1987, pp. 298–301.

24 Cruickshanks, *Political Untouchables*, p. 29

25 *Lockhart Papers*, I, pp. 197–9, 224–5.

26 H. T. Dickinson, *Liberty and Property. Political Ideology in Eighteenth Century Britain*, 1977, pp. 53–6.

27 Sedgwick, *House of Commons*, I, pp. 62–75; Bennett, *Tory Crisis*, pp. 206–22. But, cf. Colley, *In Defiance*, pp. 236–62.

28 *Dictionary of National Biography*, VI, pp. 101–2.

29 Lenman, *Jacobite Risings*, pp. 256–7.

30 Monod, *Jacobitism*, pp. 97–101, 339.

31 Hopkins, *Glencoe*, pp. 107–8, 126, 138, etc.; Lenman, *Jacobite Risings*, p. 143; McLynn, *Charles Edward Stuart*, pp. 111–12.

32 Bossy, *English Catholic Community*, pp. 149–68 *passim*; *Affairs of Scotland*, p. 38.

33 P. K. Monod, 'The politics of matrimony: Jacobitism and marriage in eighteenth-century England', in Cruickshanks and Black, *Jacobite Challenge*, pp. 24–41.

34 Monod, *Jacobitism*, pp. 143, 183, 227.

35 Ibid., pp. 213, 214, 216, 335, 338–9; E. Mallet, *A History of the University of Oxford, Volume III, Modern Oxford*, 1927, p. 41; N. Rogers, 'Riot and popular Jacobitism in early Hanoverian England', in Cruickshanks, *Ideology and Conspiracy*, pp. 71, 81, 84; and Rogers, 'Popular Jacobitism in provincial context: eighteenth-century Bristol and Norwich', in Cruickshanks and Black, *Jacobite Challenge*, pp. 127, 129, 132; S. Bamford, *The Autobiography of Samuel Bamford, Volume One: Early Days, Together With an Account of the Arrest, &c*, ed. W. H. Chaloner, 1967, p. 18.

36 Rogers, 'Riot and popular Jacobitism', p. 80; Monod, *Jacobitism*, 295–301.

37 Ibid., pp. 47–8, 70–94.

38 Ibid., pp. 15–44 *passim*.

39 P. K. Monod, 'Dangerous merchandise: smuggling, Jacobitism, and commercial culture in southeast England, 1690–1760', *Journal of British Studies*, XXX, 1991, pp. 150–82 *passim*; C. Winslow, 'Sussex smugglers', in D. Hay, P. Linebaugh, J. G. Rule, E. P. Thompson and C. Winslow, *Albion's Fatal Tree. Crime and Society in Eighteenth-Century England*, repr. 1988, pp. 119–66.

40 For example Francis Atterbury, Henry Sacheverell and Thomas Carte. See also, Monod, *Jacobitism*, pp. 147–53.

41 Lenman, 'Scottish episcopal clergy', pp. 44–7; *Affairs of Scotland*, pp. 8, 9–10.

2

The ideology of Jacobitism

Ideology, in the sense of a body of ideas used in support of a political theory, enables political movements to draw to themselves strangers who in other circumstances might never find common ground. Thus the simple fact that all Jacobites, from plebeian rioters bawling slogans at Whig magistrates to patrician pamphleteers seeking to undermine the Hanoverian regime by penning a dialogue between an 'honest Country Whig' and a Walpolean Whig placeman, were drawing on a common fund of ideas and beliefs is of considerable significance. If it had not developed an embracing, attractive ideology, and one suited to the political and social mores of the contemporary British Isles, Jacobitism must soon have withered and died. The content of this pattern of beliefs and values, and the way it grew and developed, is therefore of vital importance to understanding how the Jacobite cause sustained its struggle against the status quo for over sixty years.

With this in mind, what follows below falls into three parts. The first is an examination of the growth and elaboration of the formal Jacobite agenda, in other words the commitments officially entered into by the Stuart shadow-monarchs. The second looks at the ideas and motifs that provided the dynamics of popular Jacobitism. Finally, the third part of the chapter considers the 'religion' of Jacobitism, or how commitment to the cause became a moral imperative in and of itself.

The unfolding of the Jacobite ideal

Like Whiggism and Republicanism before it, Jacobitism developed a full programme of promises in the wilderness.[1] Though they were of course designed to draw support from groups believed to be sympathetic, the pattern and texture of these promises expressed something deeper about the Jacobite cause. Because James II and James 'III' truly believed in abiding by commitments solemnly entered into, the promises the exiled monarchs were coaxed or cajoled into making tell us a great deal about who was in the ascendant in the Jacobite movement at the time a given manifesto was issued.[2] And it is interesting to observe in this context the gathering radicalism of the Jacobites' political agenda. For all the innate social and political conservatism of its hard-core supporters in the British Isles, Jacobitism was impelled toward greater and greater political radicalism as time went on (see document 7).

The immediate response of the exiled dynasty and their supporters to the Revolution was a near-blind revanchism. James II's incomprehension of his Protestant subjects' hopes and fears had played a large part in precipitating the Revolution. Nonetheless he and the Catholic coterie with which he surrounded himself at St Germain soon recreated the introverted counsels that had led to his expulsion from Britain. In particular, the efficient but hated Earl of Melfort reassumed, and soon redoubled, his former influence over his royal master.[3] The formal declarations of policy produced by this council were correspondingly uncompromising. They amounted to little more than a summons to James's erstwhile subjects to return to their duty, with the threat of condign punishment if they did not (see document 1).[4] The opening battles of the propaganda war as a result went decisively in favour of the new order. Most dramatically, receipt of a threatening letter from Melfort destroyed a promising Jacobite–loyalist front that the Earl of Balcarres and Viscount Dundee were building up in the Scottish Parliament, leaving James's adherents little choice but to acquiesce in the Revolution or quietly go home and rebel.[5]

James and Melfort's intransigence was based on their assessment of the military situation. Given France's military ascendancy on the Continent between 1689 and 1692, the presence of a sizeable Jacobite army in Ireland from 1689 to 1691 and the concurrent Highland rebellion in Scotland, the court of St Germain had reason to hope that James would soon be restored by a military reconquest of the British Isles. Thus James did not feel the need to make concessions. He was supported in this by the so-called 'Noncompounder' faction within the Jacobite movement. These opposed James's 'compounding' or making concessions. Despite the presence of a handful of Protestant eccentrics in their ranks, it is apparent that the uncompromising policies advocated by this group stemmed largely from the fact that it was overwhelmingly Catholic. As such, it had everything to lose, in terms of authority at the exiled court (where Catholics were in the majority apart from a few eccentric individuals like Ailesbury and the Anglican theologian John Kettlewell) and hope for the future, if James was forced to conciliate his overwhelmingly Protestant supporters in the British Isles. Conversely, the factional counterpart of this Catholic party – the 'Compounders' – who were strong in Britain but weak at the exiled court, were so uniformly Protestant that this writer at least has been unable to find a single Catholic in their ranks.[6] The struggle between these parties for control of Jacobite policy-making erupted spasmodically for nearly four years (1689 to 1693), with the Catholics pretty much in the ascendant until at least 1692.

In the winter of 1692–3, however, Louis XIV intervened on behalf of the Protestant party, with a view to making James II more palatable to his putative subjects and thus undermining England's attachment to the Grand Alliance – which was giving France a hard time on the Continent.[7] James eventually caved in to Louis' pressure, appointed the Earl of Middleton (a Protestant) joint Secretary of State alongside the Catholics Melfort and Caryll, and issued a manifesto that represented a watershed in Jacobite thinking about the shape of a future religious and political settlement. Parliament was assigned a constitutional position very similar to that already prevailing in England in the 1690s, the religious settlement was to be left virtually untouched (the privileged position of the Church of England was specifically to be upheld) and there was to be a complete indemnity for all supporters of the Revolution and their heirs. The Irish Catholics were also to be left to the tender mercies of the first post-restoration English Parliament (see document 3). In sum, the Jacobite government-in-exile committed itself to leaving the existing political, religious and social order virtually intact in the event of a restoration.

Despite a subsequent crisis of conscience about his commitment to uphold the Church of England in all its power and glory, James II reluctantly adhered to the policies outlined in the 1693 declaration, and his son even slightly expanded the scope of the concessions on offer in 1702.[8] From 1707 onwards, however, a radical shift in the nature of the official Jacobite agenda began. The change was precipitated by the increasingly close alliance between the Jacobite and Scottish patriot cause. The Union of 1707 was one of the most sordid political 'jobs' of the eighteenth century.[9] And as a result of the lies, corruption and machinations necessary to force the incorporating Union the government in London wanted through the Scottish Parliament, a large minority (at the very least) of the Scottish political nation was left embittered and angry. The Jacobite court, despite some private sympathy with the thinking underlying the Union[10], seized the opportunity to appeal to this alienated group in 1708 and subsequently with the promise of a restoration of Scotland's independence in the event of a Jacobite victory.[11] Even though Charles Edward fudged the issue when he had the opportunity to declare Scotland's ties with England loosed in 1745 (probably out of concern for the impact of such a declaration on English public opinion), it remained an official plank in the Jacobite platform throughout the period 1707–66.[12]

Jacobitism's subsuming of the Scottish national cause was the beginning of a trend. As the Jacobites sought allies more and more amongst the politically alienated and dispossessed, so they accumulated more and more commitments to alter the status quo in the event of a restoration. Thus a full, formal commitment to religious toleration, even for Catholics, began to reappear in Jacobite manifestos from 1715 onwards.[13] To appreciate the significance and radicalism of this proposal it is only necessary to reflect that this was an issue no conventional politician would touch before the 1770s, that it convulsed British politics in 1780, 1799–1800 and 1825–9 and brought down at least two governments before it was finally passed. From the mid-1720s too, promises to roll back the systematic manipulation of borough franchises by the Whig regime and reverse the disfranchisement of plebeian Londoners by Walpolean legislation designed to boost the powers of the ministerially dominated court of Aldermen, began to feature regularly in Jacobite propaganda. Most significantly of all, the Jacobite court pledged it would hold a 'Free Parliament'. This had been a radical nostrum since the 1650s, bound to appeal to anyone who felt they had been unjustly treated by the existing order.[14] The denouement of this process came in the 1750s, when Charles Edward planned to commit the exiled dynasty to biannual or triannual Parliaments, disbanding the standing army, cutting the number of placemen in Parliament to no more than 50 and enacting legal guarantees of the liberty of the press and the right of the people to resist tyrannical governments (see document 7). It was an agenda most late-eighteenth-century radicals would have enthusiastically endorsed. Furthermore, in and of itself a Jacobite restoration would inevitably have realigned Britain diplomatically and led to a withdrawal from European commitments many radicals later blasted as iniquitous.

Popular Jacobitism and its motifs

Predictably, the formal pronouncements of the Jacobite court only indirectly related to the discourse and motifs of popular Jacobitism. The language of the crowd and the poetry and other ephemera of their betters stemmed not from such official statements but from more ancient traditions of loyalism and resistance with which Jacobitism became aligned. Given its longevity this is not surprising, as by the 1720s there would have been few plebeians or patricians disenchanted with the current order who could remember another discourse of opposition. Nonetheless, the fervour with which plebeian and patrician Jacobites expressed their sentiments is striking – and the impact is redoubled when the consequences of speaking, writing or acting against the Hanoverian regime are borne in mind.[15]

Popular loyalism was a feature of plebeian culture throughout the early modern period, and it was not to be expected that Britain's lower orders would wholly transfer their affections to a new dynasty while a scion of the old one still lived.[16] William and Mary seem to have sidestepped the problem because they were both Stuarts by descent and William was in addition the Protestant hero who had saved England from popery.[17] The Hanoverians, however, faced it in full force. Queen Anne enjoyed enormous personal popularity because she was a quintessentially Anglican, paternalistic monarch.[18] The uncharismatic George I was by contrast a manifestly *foreign* monarch who spoke poor English and had no time for the cherished popular traditions the Stuarts had upheld, the best known being touching for the king's evil.[19] To make matters worse, he was believed to be uncompromisingly aligned with the Whigs, who were not popular in 1714. A significant section of the English crowd responded by asserting their customary loyalism in Jacobite forms. The period 1715–20 is thus full of crowds proclaiming the Old Pretender, singing Jacobite songs (the old Cavalier anthem 'The King shall enjoy his own again' was the most popular), pointedly wearing oak leaves on 29 May to signify their adherence to the Stuarts and flaunting white roses on the Old Pretender's birthday. They also, on occasion, attacked Whigs celebrating anniversaries stemming from their traditional calendar, broke the windows of or roughed up individuals who refused to participate in their festivities and fought troops loyal to the regime who were trying to reimpose order.[20] From the 1720s some of the fire went out of this militant plebeian Jacobitism, but plebeian demonstrations of loyalty to the Stuarts continued to crop up occasionally into the 1750s.

Patrician loyalism was generally expressed in less physical forms than plebeian, but in its own way it was just as graphic. Drinking the Old Pretender's health upon their knees was a commonplace of patrician Jacobite festivities in the early eighteenth century, and the later custom of drinking to the health of the (unnamed) king while carefully holding one's glass over a bowl of water (i.e. drinking the health of the king over the water – James 'III') only looks quaint to twentieth-century eyes. Likewise the wearing of tartan waistcoats in the late 1740s, hanging unlabelled portraits of the exiled Stuart royal family in their country houses and penning and reading poetry evoking the good old days of lost (Stuart) innocence.

> Thus when rebellious angels fell,
> The very heav'n, where good ones dwell,
> Became th'apostate spirits' hell.
>
> Seeking against eternal right,
> A force without a love and light,
> They found and felt its evil might.
>
> Thus Adam biting at their bait,
> Of good and evil when he ate,
> Died to his first thrice happy state

lamented the Jacobite poet John Byrom.[21] A major motif in eight-eenth-century poetry, that of the 'lost lover', stemmed directly from this patrician Jacobitism.[22]

Popular Jacobitism was, of course, not all always as seemly as might be inferred from the motifs outlined above. Jacobitism was undoubtedly the major motivating force for many members of the plebeian crowd, but for at least as many others it was simply the language of opposition. If you really wanted to annoy your betters between 1715 and 1750, particularly those in the magistracy, the most effective way to do it was to poke fun at the Hanoverian dynasty. It was an easy mark. George I's marital problems led to endless songs and doggerel on the venerable subject of cuckolds:

> Came ye o'er frae France?
> Came ye doun by Lunnon?
> Saw ye Geordie Whelps
> And his bonny woman?
> Were ye at the place
> Ca'd the Kittle Housie?
> Saw ye Geordie's grace
> Riding on a goosie?
>
> Geordie he's a man,
> There is little doubt o't;
> He's done a' he can,
> Wha can do without it?
> Down there came a blade,
> Linkin like my lordie;
> He wad drive a trade
> At the loom o'Geordie.[23]

Every time a Jacobite crowd constructed an effigy of him for hanging or burning he was depicted with the customary horns. His taste in mistresses – they were nicknamed 'the Goose' and 'the Elephant' – was also ridiculed in song and mime. By extension the legitimacy of George II was questioned over and over again in demonstrations and ribald ballads.[24]

The most important manifestation of popular Jacobitism from the point of view of sustaining the cause was its growing identification with the common people's long-cherished hopes of the onset of a redeemer. In effect the Old Pretender assumed some of the aspects of King Arthur in the minds of many of his plebeian adherents. He was cast as the good king who would one day return and put all things right.[25] This idea is most apparent as an undertone in many songs that were popular with plebeian audiences during the period, and more starkly laid out in the secret societies of the Irish countryside. As late as the 1790s the Defenders (a plebeian Catholic secret society) were still swearing in new members with oaths that pledged them to fight to restore the Stuarts so that the dispossessed, i.e. the Catholics, could reclaim what was rightfully theirs.[26] More elegantly, the thrust of the 'lost lover' genre of poetry was that social harmony would be restored with the Old Pretender (and after 1745, by Charles Edward). James's popular image correspondingly reflected the belief that he represented the 'right' kind of king. Thus he was presented as dining on English beef and drinking – in moderation – good English ale even though he was living far away in Rome, as well as being a man with no time for the fripperies of the decadent and corrupt regime in Britain.[27] And in his people's hour of greatest need, by implication, he would come and rescue them from their oppressors.

The religion of Jacobitism

All long-running political movements accumulate a tradition which they lovingly preserve. Victories are fondly recalled, defeats sadly mourned, heroes celebrated and martyrs remembered. Because it endured for so long, Jacobitism accumulated a veritable baggage train in this respect. And as the generations passed and any realistic hope of a restoration faded, the introversion of the shrinking hard core of Jacobites deepened and the observance of this uniquely Jacobite calendar became in effect a neo-religious act distinct and separate from the confessional attachments the Jacobites variously observed.[28]

A powerful component in the religion of Jacobitism was a profound reverence for its martyred dead. With a few exceptions, such as the young apprentice James Shepherd, who was executed for fantasising about killing George I, most Jacobite martyrs died in batches after the failure of conspiracies or risings. They were all publicly executed, and in accord with the custom of the time were allowed to address the crowd from the scaffold or the ladder by the gallows. Criminals generally used, or were persuaded by the clergymen ministering to them to use, this last opportunity to speak to their fellow subjects to reinforce the normative values of society. Thus they would admit their guilt, endorse the justice of their sentence, warn the crowd against taking up the sinful ways that had led them to their final sorry pass and beg forgiveness of their kinsmen, neighbours and fellow subjects before being, in contemporary parlance, 'turned off'.[29] The overwhelming majority of Jacobites absolutely refused to play this game. When given the opportunity to address the crowd assembled to watch them die, they instead denied they were guilty of rebellion or treason against their lawful king, praised the exiled royal family, excoriated the Hanoverian regime and exhorted their kinsmen, neighbours and fellow subjects to rebel against the Hanoverian usurper (see documents 2 and 6).[30] The authorities seem to have been non-plussed, and made only half-hearted efforts to silence the torrent of sedition that was flowing from their most solemn demonstration of power. As a result, the vast majority of the 200 or so executions for conspiracy or rebellion 1689–1752 became heroic episodes in Jacobite lore. In a sense, by turning their final moments into an exultant vindication of the cause they were dying for, men like Sir John Ashton and Archibald Cameron were not only subverting the customary theatre of death, they were transmitting their values to the next generation in the most powerful way possible.[31]

Consequently, the sub-culture of the Jacobite milieu developed a special reverence for its martyrs. 'Blessed are those who suffer for righteousness' sake', was a text quoted over and over again by Jacobites about to die; their fellow Jacobites agreed and acted accordingly. The dying speeches of ordinary Jacobites were assidu-ously collected and preserved by a wide spectrum of country squires, clergymen and urban bourgeoisie. Pictures of those who had suffered the final penalty were hung in Jacobite political clubs and country houses. Alongside the classic memorabilia of Jacobitism – knick-knacks and gifts associated with Bonnie Prince Charlie or received from the hand of James II or James 'III' – martyr's 'relics' increasingly featured. The Walton-le-dale 'corpor-ation', a High Tory–Jacobite political club, lovingly preserved a short stave presented by the young, handsome and tragic Earl of Derwentwater, who was executed in 1716.[32] His grave became a place of pilgrimage for local plebeian Jacobites.[33] In the same vein the Nonjuring Bishop Richard Rawlinson had his heirs bury him with a skull under his right hand which he believed to be that of Christopher Layer, executed for conspiring to overthrow George I in 1722. Another Jacobite, Edward Hall, was honoured ever after for a night-time raid on the gates of Manchester in 1748 to retrieve the heads of those executed following the failure of the '45.[34]

What is as striking about these instances as the Jacobites' concern with preserving the memory of their martyrs is their apparent imperviousness to the impact of the executions on society at large. The trial, condemnation and execution of Jacobites signalled *failure* to the mass of the population of the British Isles, however much the crowds surrounding the scaffolds admired their courage in the face of death. It is thus a measure of the introversion of the Jacobite milieu that its sub-culture was able blithely to ignore the general reaction, and ultimate rejection of them and their cause among the population as a whole, as a result of the phenomenon they revered so highly.

Notes

1 See for example: HMC Stuart Papers, I, pp. 218–21: 'James VIII to his good people of his ancient Kingdom of Scotland', St Germain, 1 March 1708 (ns); Stuart Papers, Box 6/26: 'His Majesty's Most Gracious Declaration', Pezzaro, 21 March 1717 (ns).

2 D. Szechi, 'The Jacobite Revolution Settlement 1689–1696', *English Historical Review*, CVIII, 1993, pp. 610–28 *passim*.

3 F. C. Turner, *James II*, repr. 1950, pp. 458–9.

4 Bodleian Library, Oxford, MS Carte 181, ff. 424r–424ar: 'By the King. A Proclamation', Dublin, 1 April 1689.

5 Hopkins, *Glencoe*, pp. 126–7. For the text of the letter, see the document below.

6 Szechi, 'Revolution Settlement', pp. 613–14.

7 Ibid., pp. 619–26; J. Childs, *The Nine Years War and the British Army 1688–1697. The Operations in the Low Countries*, Manchester, 1991, p. 214.

8 J. S. Clarke, ed., *The Life of James the Second, King of England, &c, Collected Out of Memoirs Writ of His Own Hand*, 2 vols., 1816, II, pp. 508–16; J. J. Macpherson, ed., *Original Papers. Containing the Secret History of Great Britain From the Restoration to the Accession of the House of Hannover*, 2 vols., 1775, II, pp. 606–7.

9 W. Ferguson, *Scotland's Relations With England. A Survey to 1707*, Edinburgh, 1977, pp. 232–66.

10 MS Carte 180, ff. 349–50: Middleton to the Old Pretender, St Germain, 1711.

11 HMC Stuart, I, p. 219: 'James VIII to . . . Scotland', 1 March 1708 (ns).

12 McLynn, *Charles Edward Stuart*, p. 163; Stuart Papers 254/93: 'His Majesty's Most Gracious Declaration', 23 December 1743 ns.

13 Stuart Papers Box 6/26: 'His Majesty's . . . Declaration', 21 Mar. 1717 (ns)

14 Plumb, *Political Stability*, pp. 159–87; Stuart Papers 254/92: 'His Majesty's Most Gracious Declaration' (for England), 23 December 1743 ns; 254/94: 'His Majesty's Most Gracious Declaration' (for London), 23 December 1743 (ns).

15 See for example the fates of John Matthews and Thomas Cooke, Monod, *Jacobitism*, pp. 39–40, 262.

16 D. M. Loades, *Politics and the Nation 1450–1660*, 3rd, revised, edn, 1986, pp. 221–3; L. Colley, *Britons. Forging the Nation 1707–1837*, 1992, pp. 202–36.

17 S. B. Baxter, *William III and the Defense of European Liberty 1650–1702*, 1966, p. 401.

18 Gregg, *Queen Anne*, p. 153.

19 R. M. Hatton, *George I. Elector and King*, 1978, pp. 130–40, 165, 171–3.

20 Monod, *Jacobitism*, pp. 173–95.

21 R. Lonsdale, ed., *The New Oxford Book of Eighteenth Century Verse*, Oxford, 1987, pp. 213–14: 'On the origin of evil'; Pittock, *Invention of Scotland*, pp. 24, 51.

22 National Library of Wales, Penrice and Margam MSS, L695: ?to Sir Thomas Mansel, 3 November (1710); Monod, *Jacobitism*, pp. 49–69, 199, 289–90; Pittock, *Invention of Scotland*, p. 46.

23 G. S. Macquoid, ed., *Jacobite Songs and Ballads*, 1887, pp. 64–5: 'Came ye o'er frae France'. The 'blade' referred to in the second verse is Count Konigsmark, George's alleged cuckolder. See also, *Autobiography of Samuel Bamford*, p. 21.

24 Rogers, 'Riot and popular Jacobitism', pp. 71–2.

25 Monod, *Jacobitism*, pp. 62–7; *Autobiography of Samuel Bamford*, p. 21.

26 R. F. Foster, *Modern Ireland 1600–1972*, 1989, pp. 271, 279.

27 *Somerset and Dorset Notes and Queries*, XXIII, 1939–42, p. 272, also quoted in W. Michael, *England Under George I. The Quadruple Alliance*, 1939, pp. 205–6.

28 Alongside an increasingly mystical exaltation of the place of the Nonjuring churches in God's cosmic plan, and a tendency to conflate the sufferings of the Stuarts and the passion of Christ. Pittock, *Invention of Scotland*, pp. 10, 24, 30–1, 47.

29 J. A. Sharpe, ' "Last dying speeches": religion, ideology and public execution in seventeenth-century England', *Past and Present*, CVII, 1985, pp. 144–63.

30 See for example, *True Copies, passim*.

31 D. Szechi, 'The Jacobite theatre of death', in E. Cruickshanks and J. Black, eds., *The Jacobite Challenge*, Edinburgh, 1988, pp. 57–73, and see below, pp. 148–50.

32 Monod, *Jacobitism*, pp. 285, 288, 289–91, 299.

33 HMC Stuart, II, p. 84: Hugh Thomas to (David Nairne), 2 April 1716.

34 Monod, *Jacobitism*, pp. 300, 306.

3

Jacobitism and the British
state, 1689–1716

As the principal opponent of the established order in the British
Isles for the best part of a century, Jacobitism could not fail to have
a major impact on the development of the British state. The threat,
real or imagined, of Jacobite-inspired insurrection or Jacobite-
assisted foreign invasion periodically dominated the deliberations
of Britain's rulers, generally limited their policy options and always
restricted the range of their political choices. Consequently any
survey of the Jacobite cause must concern itself at some point with
the British state's response to the Jacobite 'menace'. What follows,
then, is a brief overview of how its confrontation with Jacobitism
affected this, in contemporary terms very powerful, state's growth
in one of its most formative periods: from the early 1690s, when
it was urgently overhauled to wage the Nine Years War at home
and abroad, up to the securing of the established order by the
defeat of the 1715 rebellion.[1]

The struggle for the periphery, 1689–1691

One of the few objectives of William of Orange's invasion of
England in 1688 of which we can be certain was his intention to
harness England's resources to the war-effort against France about
to be mounted by the Grand Alliance. The English political nation,
however, naturally regarded its own security, and England's traditional hegemony within the British Isles, as more important than
the needs of its new monarch's allies on the Continent.[2] A vital first
step in persuading the English political nation that the new regime

should be allowed to focus England's potential on the Continental struggle with France was then, the elimination of the threat posed by Jacobite loyalists in Scotland and Ireland.

Neither kingdom could of itself have deployed sufficient forces seriously to assault the Williamite regime in England. Both were capable, however, of being used as platforms from which to launch a French invasion – provided the French could build up sufficient forces there. Since William's successful invasion had caught the French strategically off balance, with the bulk of their forces already committed to the war in Flanders and on the Rhine,[3] he had the opportunity to neutralise the Jacobites in Scotland and Ireland before French intervention could realise the potential threat. Rather than risk losing the small army he had brought with him, William therefore tried to negotiate a quick settlement with the magnates who had seized control of Edinburgh and James II's former lieutenant, the Earl of Tyrconnell, in Ireland.

The Scots magnates, political chieftains like the Marquess of Atholl and the Duke of Hamilton, had almost all been alienated by the Drummond brothers' zealously Catholic conduct of affairs well before 1688. Brought back into government during the crisis of that autumn, they were looking to consolidate their newly regained ascendancy from the outset, and correspondingly seized the first opportunity they could to come to terms with William. He was thus able, at least superficially, to take control of Scotland at the beginning of March 1689.[4] There remained, however, a strong body of Jacobite loyalists at large among the political nation. By mid-March this group was rapidly coalescing into an action party centred on Viscount Dundee, and a more inchoate and diffuse Episcopalian loyalist interest that was withholding support from the new regime, but was as yet reluctant to enter into a violent confrontation.[5] Prompt government action at the end of the month resulted in the arrest of the Earl of Mar and the cowing of most of the rest of the loyalist interest, except for the most dangerous of them all, Dundee, who evaded his pursuers and escaped to the Highlands.

By contrast with Hamilton and his ilk, Tyrconnell was a political insider with a lot to lose if the new order took control of Ireland. His initial reaction to William's seizure of power was concomitantly cautious: he opened negotiations on the basis of a return to the religio-political status quo operating at the time of James's accession. Since he must have been well aware this was unlikely to be acceptable to either Protestants or Catholics in Ireland, we can only surmise that he was playing for time. It is certain that while William was trying to win him over, Tyrconnell was building up his forces and preparing to fight.[6] War in any case became inevitable when James and a bevy of French officers landed at Kinsale on 12 March 1689. He was looking to use Ireland as a stepping-stone back to England from the very start,[7] and in and of himself represented a challenge to William's authority the usurper could not ignore.

For a short time, however, James's return seemed to give his supporters the initiative in the oncoming conflict. In Ireland James, somewhat unwillingly, found himself leading a revanchist Catholic Irish crusade, determined to wrest religious toleration and some degree of independence from Westminster from any future political settlement in the British Isles. The Dublin Parliament of 1689's apparent ambition to free itself from English tutelage has subsequently won it a place in the nationalist mythology of Ireland. Actually, it was riven by feuding between the Old English and the Old Irish, and was primarily concerned with overturning the Restoration land settlement, which had legitimised the reduction of Catholic landownership to c.21 per cent of the total.[8] While it squabbled, and James vainly tried to restrain the enthusiasm of the Catholic clergy for repossessing church buildings from their Protestant tenants,[9] the French commanders he had brought with him got on with the siege of the predominantly Presbyterian town of Londonderry. At the same time in Scotland official commissions from James gave Dundee sufficient leverage to persuade some of the clan chieftains to support a rising in James's name in the Highlands.[10] Only a tiny army of barely a thousand men mustered on 18 May 1689, but it was more than the beleaguered, already faction-ridden, Williamite governors of Scotland could cope with.

With his partisans' positions in both Scotland and Ireland clearly under threat from a Jacobite counter-offensive (however feeble it may seem in retrospect), William had little choice but to commit himself to rescuing them, even at the cost of his Continental strategy. The English professional standing army had almost completely disintegrated over the winter of 1688–9, so his government's first task was to rebuild it.[11] In the interim, massive subsidies had to be extracted from the fractious English Parliament in order to buy the services of Danish and German auxiliaries. Given the innate resistance of all seventeenth-century English Parliaments to making large grants of taxation this inevitably turned into a protracted and ill-tempered process.[12] Meanwhile, the Williamites' situation in Scotland and Ireland steadily worsened.

In May 1689 Dundee led his little army on its first raid into the lowlands. After various fruitless manoeuvres, feints and retreats over the next two months he finally got a chance to attack the main Williamite force under Major-General Hugh Mackay at the pass of Killiecrankie. There Dundee scored one of the most unexpected victories of the war before metamorphosing gloriously into the archetype of the Jacobite martyr-hero by getting himself shot dead in the final stages of the battle.[13] Though the rebel army's progress was checked at the 'battle' of Dunkeld shortly afterwards, Mackay's defeat ensured the rising took root among the Jacobite clans. From the summer of 1689 a bitter war of raid and counter-raid accordingly developed in and around the Highlands.[14] Lowland militia levies and friendly clans could, and did, carry a large part of the burden of containing the insurrection, but they were only capable of blocking and harrassing it, not of suppressing it at source. As the New Model Army had discovered in the 1650s, the only way to put down a rebellion in the Highlands was to maintain strong garrisons in the glens themselves. These would then raid and destroy the Highlanders' homes and crops year-round until the rebel clansmen grew tired of the unequal struggle and submitted. Only regular troops, professionally commanded and maintained by expensive supply lines were capable of this kind of sustained, brutal warfare. The Williamite regime in Scotland possessed neither the political weight, nor, one suspects, the political will to find the money to pay for such expensive military operations, so William and his ministers in London were obliged to find the necessary men and resources south of the border.[15]

From the autumn of 1689 William and his ministers began diverting a steady dribble of troops and money from the other war-fronts into Scotland. The first substantial success of Williamite arms duly followed in May 1690, when a revitalised Jacobite host led by Major-General Thomas Buchan was routed at the Haughs of Cromdale.[16] This served to put the rebellion firmly on the defensive, and for the rest of the year the government steadily built up its forces in the old fortresses that dominated the crossroads of the Highlands. From these bases the army relentlessly harried the Jacobite clans throughout the winter and spring of 1690–1. The rapine and destruction finally forced the Jacobites to agree to a truce in June 1691 while the chieftains sent emissaries to ask James II's permission to submit to the Williamite regime. Both sides well knew that the truce signalled the end of the war in Scotland. The emissaries were primed to demand James's 'permission' to surrender if he could not offer the clans immediate reinforcements from France – which they were well aware he could not.[17] With the war in Ireland manifestly coming to a close there was in any case no point in Scotland's Jacobites fighting on in lonely, futile isolation.

The Jacobite war in Ireland was wholly different from the Highland war in Scotland. From the outset statesmen on both sides were a great deal more committed to winning the war there than in Scotland. Except at certain crucial junctures Scotland could never be more than a sideshow for William and his ministers and their Jacobite counterparts. By contrast, Ireland's large Catholic population appeared to offer the possibility of its acting as the powerhouse for a counter-revolution, and both sides therefore felt compelled to take the war there very seriously. In psychological terms too, victory in Ireland was more urgent than victory in Scotland. During the course of the seventeenth century its overwhelmingly Catholic population had become the principal focus of English paranoia about the popish menace.[18] The horrors of the massacres of Protestant settlers in Ulster that prefaced the Irish rebellion of 1641 had been told and retold, exaggerated and amplified for nearly half a century by the time of the Jacobite war in Ireland, and any English government that failed to rescue the beleaguered Protestants of the western kingdom was liable to fail politically in England too.

In between organising and despatching Mackay's army to Scotland and the remains of the old English standing army to Flanders under the Earl of Marlborough, negotiating new taxes and a constitutional settlement with an aggressively assertive English Parliament and intervening diplomatically to maintain the unity and coherence of the Grand Alliance, William and his ministers had then to construct some kind of strategy for 'saving' Ireland's Protestants. Following the defeat of Lord Mountalexander and a scratch force of Protestants at the Break of Dromore in mid-March 1689, the area under Williamite control had, moreover, shrunk to that surrounding the two remaining bastions controlled by

Ulster's Protestant settlers: Londonderry and Enniskillen, and Londonderry was under close siege by mid-April.[19] The Williamites' situation in Ireland was clearly getting desperate. In the circumstances, the English government's piecemeal response to the crisis is not in the least surprising: relief and reinforcements were sent to Ireland as they became available, rather than in any coordinated and rational fashion, and, as is the way of such responses, they met with very mixed success.

Admiral Herbert's attempts to drive off the French fleet and the reinforcements it was carrying ignominiously failed when he was defeated at the battle of Bantry Bay at the end of April.[20] Major-General Kirke's efforts to break through to Londonderry were finally successful at the end of July, and shortly afterwards the Williamite defenders of Enniskillen heavily defeated a Jacobite force at Newtownbutler.[21] The Duke of Schomberg and a polyglot army of raw English troops and hard-bitten European mercenaries followed this up by landing in eastern Ulster in mid-August. Well out on a logistical limb, however, Schomberg advanced only cautiously southwards towards Dublin, and when confronted at Dundalk by James II himself at the head of a Jacobite army, prudently declined to fight, thereby allowing the Jacobite regime still more time to consolidate its hold on the rest of the country.[22] Over the winter of 1689–90, however, the balance of forces dramatically shifted in favour of the Williamites. The Royal Navy regained control of the Irish Sea, and a proper logistical and supply network was built up that steadily pumped reinforcements into Schomberg's army.[23] By the summer of 1690 Schomberg had under his command an army not much smaller than James's and a logistical infrastructure the Jacobites could not hope to match. To round it off, William himself came over in June with a further 15,000 European mercenaries. The stage was thus set for a major, Continental-style campaign in which the ill-armed and poorly trained Jacobite forces would be seriously outclassed.[24]

Prima facie there is no obvious reason why the Jacobite army could not have been built up into a force at least as formidable as that which was about to descend upon it. The Catholic Irish had responded enthusiastically to James's call to arms in 1689, and he and his generals had had plenty of time to train and prepare their raw recruits to face the Williamites. Likewise James had plenty of officers experienced in the arts of siegecraft, organisation and supply that were the crux of success and failure in late seventeenth-century warfare.[25] There was a serious shortage of modern firearms and heavy ordinance on the Jacobite side, but it was not so serious as to make more than a marginal difference between the military capabilities of the two sides. Yet the Jacobites' performance against their Williamite foes in 1690 was almost unrelievedly dismal. What went wrong?

More than anything else the failure of the Jacobite army in 1690–1 is ascribable to a failure of political will. James II does not seem to have taken to his Old Irish subjects.[26] They, in turn, were soon disillusioned with him and his inner coterie of advisers, none of whom were Old Irish;[27] hence the suspicion with which the rank-and-file and many junior officers of the Jacobite army regarded James's attempts to discipline and organise the new army along unfamiliar, Continental lines.[28] Most of the professional military officers with Continental experience who accompanied James II to Ireland were of Old English descent, and his appointment of them to virtually all the senior positions in the Jacobite army looked very like partiality to the excluded and resentful Old Irish.[29] Bickering and obstruction consequently hampered efforts to forge a modern army out of the mass of raw recruits who composed the army in 1689. James could have intervened personally to supervise the process and neutralise it politically, but seems to have lacked the drive to do so. Indeed, his whole conduct of affairs in Ireland between 1689 and 1690 was uncharacteristically hesitant, supporting the thesis that the catastrophe which struck his house in 1688 broke his nerve permanently.[30] To compound the problem, James's only ally, France, was unwilling to commit significant resources to upholding James's cause in the western kingdom. Louis XIV and his ministers saw Flanders and the Rhine as the crucial theatres of the war, with Ireland coming below Italy in order of priority after that. Thus William was prepared to go on the defensive, even lose ground, in Europe to win in Ireland but Louis was not. Consequently, while William poured his best troops and commanders into Ireland, Louis sent only a small French contingent, a mere trickle of munitions and his second-string generals.

The outcome was predictable. On 1 July 1690 William's 35,000-strong army, composed mainly of veteran professionals, crushed its 24,000–strong Jacobite rival in a bruising, unimaginative soldiers' battle while forcing the river Boyne.[31] Within three days James was on a ship back to France, lamenting his fate and blaming the disaster on his Irish subjects. Their feelings towards him after his flight are summarised in the nickname he subsequently acquired from the Old Irish bards: 'Séamus an chaca' ('James the beshitten').[32] Even so, the war was not over. William quickly took Dublin and pushed on westward to besiege Limerick, the key to control of western Ireland. There he was conclusively checked by a Jacobite rally inspired in equal parts by the French naval victory at Beachy Head and the charisma of the dashing Patrick Sarsfield.[33]

William's swift advance away from his bases in the east and north of the island had already strained his supply lines, and the valiant resistance put up by Limerick's defenders added to the problem by forcing William to settle down for a regular siege using heavy artillery. This, along with the engineers and munitions necessary to use it effectively had to be transported across Ireland along the already overburdened roads. Sarsfield's cavalry raids against artillery and supply trains hopelessly compounded William's problems, and he was forced to lift the siege after less than a month.[34] Hope accordingly revived on the Jacobite side, but a more sombre conclusion would have been appropriate given the outcome of events elsewhere in Ireland. By concentrating virtually all its available forces on defending Limerick the Jacobite army had succeeded in forcing William's overextended army to retreat back behind the river Shannon. As William retired, however, Marlborough was already landing in Munster with an entirely independent army fresh from England, which in short order captured Cork and Kinsale.[35] English resources and the Williamite regime's determination to win the war in Ireland were proving an overwhelming combination.

Nonetheless, the Jacobite army's morale revived, and with the arrival of a new French commander, the Marquis de St Ruth, and the experience the Irish troops had gained in the school of hard knocks the previous year, there would seem superficially to have been some prospect of their holding out. The relative efficiency of the Williamite war machine, however, belied it once again. Baron von Ginkel, who now commanded the Williamite forces, was a stolid and orthodox soldier. St Ruth and Sarsfield had genuine flair. Yet they proved unable to do more than delay Ginkel's steady advance.[36] In desperation St Ruth risked everything on a roll of the dice, and at the battle of Aughrim in July 1691 lost the game. Ginkel won a hard-fought victory, then pressed on to capture Galway and lay siege to Limerick. The defence was courageous but despairing, and in September the defenders accepted Ginkel's generous surrender terms.[37] Those who wished to fight on were to be allowed to depart peacefully for France, everyone else was to be allowed to return peacefully home. The first, and most difficult, struggle between the Jacobites and the new order in the British Isles was over and the new model British state had won.

Two years of bitter civil war had secured the English Williamite regime's control of the British Isles, but the political and economic costs were enormous and lingering. Reduced to basics, the Williamites won by spending vast sums of English money on creating a modern military machine that was in large part dependent on European mercenaries. The money was raised by taxation and borrowing in England on a scale unimaginable before 1688.[38] Caught up in the need to defend the new order, which many, if not most, of the English political nation in 1689 regarded as their only defence against the kind of popish revanchism they believed James II represented (with some justice: see document 1), the English Lords and Commons reluctantly accepted the necessity for the *de facto* militarisation of the British state.[39] This does not mean they were happy with it. Many, indeed, were appalled and began to question the value of a revolution that so irrevocably broke with the comfortably unmilitary traditions of Restoration England.[40] Compounding the problem for many of the Anglican majority, who were already unhappy at having to accept a stubborn Calvinist as the supreme governor of the Church of England, was the apparent burgeoning of Protestant religious dissent after the passage of the Toleration Act of 1689.[41] In this combination of misgivings about the consequences of the Revolution and nostalgia for the 'simpler' world they had lost in 1688 lay the seeds of a Jacobite revival. In order to defeat Jacobitism militarily the new order had, in effect, created conditions that guaranteed its endurance.

If the Williamite regime in England was compromised by the measures it had to take to win the war, its stepchildren in Scotland and Ireland were doubly compromised. Unable to quell the Jacobites themselves, the Revolution interest in Scotland had been forced to call in English troops and rely on English money to secure itself in power. For all practical purposes the Scottish state had become the pensioner and agent of Westminster. In many ways, of course, this simply replicated the situation that had existed since at least 1650 and arguably since 1625. What was different was that there had been an intervening burst of rhetoric, excitement, and, amongst certain elements of the political nation, hope, of a new order in Scotland. The radical justification for the act deposing James VII – that he had 'forefaulted' himself by his conduct – proved to be the first stirring of a resurgent, militant Scottish patriotism that was increasingly to dominate the political agenda in the northern kingdom.[42] Such feelings were never universal, and in the case of most politicians were transitory, but the tiny core of Scottish politicians who genuinely did adhere to a patriotic position (as opposed to those who adopted it for tactical purposes), were both able to express themselves much more openly after 1689 as a consequence of the constitutional settlement in Scotland, and had a ready source of national grievance in the manifest subordination of the Revolution interest in Scotland to the dictates of its paymaster in England.[43] In Scotland too then, measures taken to win the war against the Jacobites planted the seeds of a future Jacobite revival.

In Ireland the subordination of the post-Revolutionary regime to the government at Westminster was even more blatant, and humiliating, than in Scotland. The rulers of Ireland after 1691, with the honourable exception of the defenders of Londonderry and Enniskillen (and, ironically, since most of them were Dissenters they were excluded from power by the terms of the religious settlement in Ireland), returned in the baggage-train of William III's army. They had been exposed as an alien garrison in hostile territory, and in the enduring climate of fear and suspicion created by the sectarian mien of the war, most seem not to have been too unhappy to continue to be treated that way once the war was over.[44] For nearly a decade Ireland was, almost literally, an occupied country, in which semi-military *coloniae*, such as the Huguenot veterans settled at Portarlington and Lisburn, were planted, and the religious and economic activities of the conquered natives watched and circumscribed.[45] The Irish Parliament initially could not, and later would not, meet the cost of maintaining the substantial army of English troops judged necessary to keep the Catholics down. Correspondingly, Ireland was rendered not just subordinate, but subservient to the vagaries of politics at

Westminster; little more than an ancillary theatre for the manoeuvrings of English politicians.[46] Hence, when a nascent Irish Patriot like William Molyneaux published a pamphlet in 1698 attacking the Irish Parliament's subordination to the English Parliament, his reward was the prompt condemnation of his ideas by the Parliament whose rights he was asserting. Nonetheless, their reduction to the status of handmaidens to the ruling clique at Westminster did have one advantage for the Williamite regime in Ireland: it guaranteed the permanent presence of a large enough English garrison (albeit theoretically on the Irish army's payroll) thoroughly to stifle any possibility of a revival of active Jacobitism. Jacobitism lodged itself close to the heart of the culture of Ireland's repressed Catholic majority for most of the eighteenth century, but it was never a military threat there again.[47] The desperate and the frustrated amongst the Catholic population slipped away to join the Irish regiments in France for the next two generations, thereby ironically helping to perpetuate the status quo that had driven them out.[48] In the sense that the Williamite victory permanently stamped out overt manifestations of support for its rival then, the conquest of Ireland 1689–91 must be regarded as a clear-cut success for the British state.

The War of the English Succession, 1689–1697

Between 1689 and 1691 winning the war in the British Isles was the top priority for William and his ministers. Yet it must not be forgotten that the struggle there was only part of a much greater conflict that raged world-wide from 1689 to 1697. In European history this war has tended to go by a number of different names: the War of the League of Augsburg; the War of the Grand Alliance; and, most popular of all, the Nine Years War. Each name implies, however gently, a particular interpretation of the conflict – hence the recent popularity of the last, most neutral, name.[49] The choice of the subheading above is thus a deliberate statement. From the point of view of the British state the war against France 1689–97 was primarily waged to secure William and Mary's usurpation of the English throne. Without France to back them the exiled Stuarts were effectively impotent between 1691 and 1715. Humbling France to the point where it would repudiate James II was therefore Britain's principal war-aim from the outset.

Late-seventeenth-century France could not be defeated by naval power. Though it had a lengthy coastline and a sizeable merchant marine – both vulnerable to the Royal Navy – it stood and fell by the fortunes of its armies. The only way to defeat France was therefore to beat its armies in the field; a contest that was bound to be bloody, lengthy and expensive. For the first time since the early sixteenth century then, Britain had to raise and deploy, supply and maintain large armies of British troops on the Continent. At the same time, Britain had to maintain a large war fleet, for while France could not be brought down by British coastal and commerce raiding, there was the distinct possibility that Britain could. No-one ever will (or can) know how many crypto-Jacobites would have rallied to James II had he landed on the south coast of England with a French army at his back in 1690, 1692 or 1696, and William and his ministers did not wish to find out. Correspondingly, the government at Westminster poured a substantial portion of its resources into expanding the Royal Navy,[50] and the Royal Navy and its Dutch allies spent most of the years 1689–92 trying to force a decisive battle on their French counterpart. The combined fleet was defeated itself at Bantry Bay and Beachy Head, and signally failed to defeat the French in several lesser actions, before it finally inflicted the decisive defeat it had been looking for at the associated battles of Barfleur and La Hogue in 1692.[51] Louis XIV and his ministers decided at that point that the strain of maintaining a substantial naval force as well as a large army was too great for France's weakening economy, and duly mothballed most of the fleet before switching over to a *guerre de course* directed against Anglo-Dutch commerce and financed by French private enterprise.[52] Thereafter, notwithstanding occasional disasters like the loss of the Smyrna convoy to French corsairs in 1693, the Anglo-Dutch fleet remained in control of the sea.

The winning of an overall dominance at sea represents one of the few clear successes scored by the Grand Alliance during the war in Europe. On land, William III consistently found himself outmanoeuvred and outclassed by his French opponents. His operational (in the sense of direct command) skills were of the 'dogged' rather than 'inspired' variety, and as a consequence the record of William's encounters with French armies is, in the main, a dreary litany of repulses and defeats. In one sense, however, these apparent setbacks were not as bad as they appeared. William was not very good at fighting battles or conducting sieges, but he was good at organising and maintaining armies. The Allied war machine he and his ministers created and directed kept going despite its miserable performance in combat. Each time the French defeated it, it steadily replaced its losses, picked itself up and reopened hostilities (at least until 1696).[53] Of course both sides' military organisations were designed to do that. The problem for France was that it was required to keep armies going on four fronts in Europe: Flanders, the Rhine, northern Italy and Catalonia. Hence the ceaseless battering of French fortresses and armies William was conducting in Flanders and coordinating with his allies on other fronts eventually wore the French down. The problem was compounded for Louis XIV by the severe harvest failure and concomitant famine which afflicted France in the mid-1690s.[54] Louis and his ministers accordingly let themselves be persuaded to accept what was in effect a losing draw. Louis recognised William as King of England and repudiated James II (though he refused to expel him from France); William agreed to stop the war.[55]

For the British state and the political nation in all three kingdoms the War of the English Succession was a traumatic experience. In Scotland and Ireland it involved sustained civil war, in England crippling taxation and repeated, humiliating defeats on the Continent. William III's credentials as the saviour of British Protestantism were unfairly, but not surprisingly, thrown into doubt by the butcher's bill at Steinkirk and Landen, and with them the revolution which had brought him to power.[56] The 1690s were thus a decade of disillusion for the political nations of all three British kingdoms, and in consequence the decade proved in the long term to be almost as valuable to the Jacobite cause as to the British state it was fighting.

The underground war, 1689–1714

The directors of the post-Revolutionary British state well knew it had many secret enemies. They sought by means of spies and informers to monitor and entrap those enemies. Conversely, the Jacobites sought to evade government surveillance while working to overthrow the Williamite regime and its successors. Thus throughout the period 1689–1759 we intermittently catch tantalising glimpses of a hidden struggle between the defenders of the new order at

Whitehall and their Jacobite antagonists in country houses, market-towns, industrial hamlets, fishing villages and taverns in all three kingdoms. What was at stake was the morale and physical security of the new order.

There were basically two ways the Jacobites could achieve their goal of overthrowing the Williamite regime and its heirs. They could rebel, i.e. openly come out in arms and march on Westminster. This approach had the virtue of simplicity. It was also tantamount to committing suicide if sufficient arms had not been gathered and distributed and sufficient supporters organised and primed to rise at the same time. Unless, moreover, such a rebellion was supported by a body of trained troops (presumably provided by a friendly foreign power) the rebels would be at a distinct disadvantage in combat with government forces.[57] Alternatively, they could sap the regime from within by means of propaganda and political manoeuvre, until it collapsed of its own accord, as had occurred in the case of the Protectorate and restored Rump in 1659–60. This was a lot safer for the individuals involved, but was necessarily a long-term process whose slow progress was liable to prove frustrating and wearisome. Both options were usually pursued simultaneously, though one was invariably emphasised more than the other at any particular time.

Military conspiracies
Between 1689 and 1714 there was a series of military-style conspiracies to restore James II. Most proved abortive, fantastic or farcical and were quietly suppressed by the Jacobites in Britain or by the exiled court at St Germain.[58] Some, like the so-called 'Lancashire' or 'Lunt' plot, were fabrications woven out of the normal round of social gatherings among groups believed (often with good cause) to be sympathetic to Jacobitism and genuine Jacobite activity stumbled upon by professional informers.[59] Three, however, stand out because they really did contain the potential to overthrow the post-Revolution regime: the inchoate conspiracy of 1691–2 that is sometimes known as the 'Ailesbury' plot, the Fenwick plot of 1695–6 and its bastard offspring the Assassination plot, and the generic conspiracy underpinning the attempted French invasion of Scotland in 1708. All these conspiracies typify the kind of approach favoured by Jacobites in Britain during the 1690s and early 1700s.

The Ailesbury plot is the name often given to a conspiratorial network organised on an *ad hoc* basis over the winter of 1691–2. The chief actors were a disparate set of peers and gentry, a significant proportion of whom were probably Catholic, whose involvement seems to have stemmed from the fact that they were known to be sympathetic to the Jacobite cause and were resident in the south of England. The Earl of Ailesbury was not actually the prime mover, but a key organiser of the plot's English end. Its originator was the Earl of Melfort, James II's principal Secretary of State, and its central feature was a French landing in southern England. The plan was that the French fleet would secure control of the English Channel long enough to convoy a substantial French army over to England with James II at its head. As soon as, or even slightly before, this invasion force landed, the English conspirators would raise their tenants, buckle on their swords and ride to meet their master.[60]

The plot got off to a good start by catching the authorities in Britain by surprise.[61] Unfortunately for the Jacobites, while the government at Westminster frantically recalled various elements of the English and Dutch fleets to oppose the threatened invasion the wind blew solidly against the French fleet, keeping it bottled up in harbour. Meanwhile Ailesbury and his fellow conspirators were being pursued and rounded up by the authorities all over southern England and troops concentrated there to oppose a landing.[62] The invasion was finally aborted in May by the Anglo-Dutch victories at Barfleur and La Hogue, but in any case would probably have been a disaster had it been attempted in the teeth of the forces the government had by then built up on the south coast.

The Fenwick plot of 1695–6 was conceived out of a combination of foolhardy optimism on the part of a network of Jacobites centred on Sir John Fenwick, and desperation on the part of Louis XIV and his ministers.[63] The plan was for Fenwick and his friends to assemble a secret force of Jacobites close by the Kentish Channel ports, where Fenwick had his main residence. On an agreed signal, in the dead of winter, the French would suddenly rush a small force from its winter quarters in northern France to the coast, embark it on a flotilla of shallow-draught invasion barges, then swiftly cross the Channel (without any warship escort) to land in Kent. There it would join up with the Fenwick rebels and stage a rapid march on London. It is a measure of the desperate

55

straits famine and the Grand Alliance's remorseless battering had reduced France to, that Louis and his ministers ever seriously contemplated this appallingly risky venture. They did, however, insist that the Fenwick plotters rise in advance of the landing and try to seize a port where the French could disembark. Due to mutual incomprehension of each other's difficulties, and some deliberate obfuscation on the part of James II and his new premier Secretary of State, the Earl of Middleton, both sides reached what was effectively an impasse on this crucial point at a very late stage in the proceedings. Everything hung fire in February 1696 because the French would not launch the invasion until the Jacobites seized a port, and the Jacobites would not rise until the French invasion landed.[64]

Meanwhile a group of adventurers on the fringes of the Fenwick plot had hatched their own ancillary operation: at the appropriate time they planned to ambush William III's coach on its way to or from his palace at Kensington. The genuine Jacobites among the plotters subsequently claimed they only intended to kidnap him, but the evidence presented by the informers who exposed the whole plot, including the Fenwick end, suggests they intended to murder him.[65] Certainly killing William would have been much easier than keeping him prisoner, which tends to validate the informers' evidence. Alerted by some suspicious gatherings of well-known Jacobites and forewarned by their informers and spies, the authorities stepped in before the plotters could act and swept up most of those involved in both the Fenwick and Assassination plots.

The French attempt to invade Scotland in 1708 was much better prepared than anything that had gone before, though, as in 1696, French support for an invasion was precipitated by a dire military emergency: the threat posed to France's northern frontiers by the smashing victories Marlborough had been winning in Flanders.[66] Between 1705 and 1707 a trusted French agent, Colonel Nathaniel Hooke (a French-naturalised Jacobite exile and convert to Catholicism), twice secretly visited Scotland, consulted with various cliques of Jacobites and other potential supporters, and took Scottish emissaries with him back to France.[67] There a plan was worked out for the transportation of a relatively small force of French troops to Scotland aboard a fleet of fast ships provided by the Dunkirk privateers. These would be greeted by a nationwide rising, and the combined forces would then drive the government's troops out of Scotland.[68] Surprise was crucial to the plan's success and it was therefore doomed as soon as the Old Pretender came down with measles just before the flotilla could sail.[69] A delay of two weeks ensued while he recovered, and when the expedition did set off it was so closely pursued by a well-prepared Royal Navy squadron that had been hovering off Dunkirk waiting for it to depart that it was unable to land the troops it carried. Despite his pleas, the French admiral would not allow the Old Pretender to go ashore alone, and insisted on withdrawing back to Dunkirk. The putative Scots rebels, who were awaiting the expedition's arrival with relish, as there were very few government troops in Scotland at the time it was due to depart, then went quietly home and denied everything.[70]

All three conspiracies have common characteristics that highlight certain general problems Jacobite conspirators always had to overcome. Rebelling without trained troops to stiffen the raw enthusiasts expected to turn out on the rebel side was generally seen as futile. Gaining the actual, physical support of a body of professional soldiers of their own was, therefore, generally regarded by rank-and-file Jacobites as a *sine qua non* of a rebellion taking place at all 1689–1714. It followed from this that the uprising in Britain and the external invasion had to be closely coordinated, so the rebels would not be exposed unsupported to government forces nor the invaders left isolated and outnumbered. Given the long delays to which contemporary communications were chronically susceptible, this was very difficult to arrange. Indeed, all the attempts to invade Britain mounted by France between 1692 and 1708 foundered on exactly that point. Finally, it is clear from the pattern of events in all three attempts/conspiracies that it was vitally necessary to catch the British government by surprise. If it had the chance to react the Royal Navy was usually capable of stopping the invasion force at sea, while the government, which had extensive knowledge of the Jacobites' networks through its spies, could (and did) quickly neutralise the conspirators in Britain by mass arrests and arms searches.

Subversion

The second option available to the Jacobites in the underground war was subversion, in the sense of undermining the moral and political bases of the new order. There were two intertwined approaches to achieving this objective: propaganda and politics.

Jacobite propaganda was a constant headache for the governments of Britain 1689–1714. Every day of every week from 1689 onwards, scurrilous lampoons of ministers, polemical tracts denouncing the moral iniquity of the post-Revolutionary social and political order and seditious ballads were being perused, read aloud, sold or sung in private houses and public places throughout Britain.[71] Given the anonymity and resilience of the small publisher, with his cheap printing press and network of street-hawkers and ballad-singers who distributed his wares, there was no possibility of the authorities ever being able entirely to stifle this Jacobite propaganda industry. They could and did harrass it by periodically tracking down and prosecuting the printers of especially obnoxious pamphlets or newspapers, or arresting the singers of seditious ballads *en masse*, but both sides knew the network would be back in operation within, at most, weeks.[72] Hence the Williamite and Augustan regimes seldom resorted to arrests and prosecutions, instead favouring counter-propaganda of various kinds, from un-officially sponsored newspapers to subsidised government hacks who would churn out 'answers' to Jacobite polemics almost as soon as they hit the streets. Interestingly enough, the inspiration for the majority of material published favouring the post-Revolution order in the British Isles can be traced back to subsidies stemming from government ministers or hacks seeking to attract favourable attention from pro-Revolution politicians.[73] By contrast, Jacobite pamphlets and ballads rarely stemmed directly from St Germain (the exiled court was suspicious of the press and anyway did not have money to 'waste' on subsidising cheap propaganda), but instead seem to have been spontaneously generated within the Jacobite community in Britain.

Jacobite political subversion arose from small groups of Tory peers and MPs in the English and Scottish, and after 1707, British Parliaments. The Irish Parliament, for obvious reasons, seems to have been untouched by Jacobite subversion. These MPs were in turn directly connected to a network of Jacobite voters and sympathisers who controlled the boroughs that returned them. There were never very many Jacobite MPs and peers in Britain's Parliaments before the Hanoverian succession (the largest number being about fifty, at most, in 1714), but they formed a vital nucleus of opposition.[74] They were inveterate opponents of the government of the day if it was primarily Whig, and a constant source of dissatisfaction and opposition within the party if it was primarily Tory. Fortunately for the Whigs and Tories who led the governments of the 1690s and 1700s, they were rarely united, and could usually be placated by concessions of a High Tory rather than Jacobite variety. Even the most intemperate of them, men like George Lockhart of Carnwath in Scotland and William Shippen in England, understood they were a minority and therefore had to achieve their ends by subterfuge. Hence, while in their own minds they were quite sure their obstruction of legislation, attacks on the post-Revolution moral order and backstairs politicking was advancing the Jacobite cause, in practical terms they tended to advance High Tory rather than Jacobite goals.[75]

The military and the subversive approaches to achieving a Jacobite restoration necessarily supported each other. The threat of a Jacobite military reconquest of the thrones of Britain obviously lent urgency to propaganda appeals for Britain's politicians to return to their duty before full-scale civil war erupted. Likewise the continued drumbeat of Jacobite accusations, libels and diatribes in print and in Parliament sustained the Jacobites' support among the general population, i.e. that section of society which would provide the cannon fodder for a rebellion. The overall impact of these two fields of Jacobite activity on the British Isles after 1691 was profound. From its nadir at Limerick in October, Jacobitism revived by 1715 to the point of being taken as the legitimate vehicle for a major national uprising in Scotland and an abortive, but potentially very threatening, party-based revolt in England. In order to understand that most important of Jacobite rebellions then, it is first necessary to review how and why Jacobitism became the idiom of opposition for both angry Scots patriots and disgruntled English Tories.

The rise of Jacobitism in England, 1692–1715

Of the three kingdoms William III and James II fought over between 1688 and 1691 there can be little doubt that England was the most disaffected to the Jacobite cause. Whereas in Scotland a small but significant part of the population rallied to his cause, and in Ireland a majority, in England the frantic efforts of loyalists like the Duke of Beaufort and Sir John Reresby were easily overmastered by their pro-Williamite opponents.[76] In late-seventeenth-century England when a great magnate like Beaufort and the commander of a major garrison like Reresby could not muster enough support to fend off a posse of Whig gentry and their servants who were engaged in arresting them, the cause they were upholding had lost all significant support.

For all practical purposes then, the English Jacobite movement began life based on an irreducible minimum of support among the political nation and the population at large. That loyalist core consisted of courtier-aristocrats like Ailesbury and Middleton (at that time both still Protestant and in England) and former officers like Sir John Fenwick, plus the Catholic community as a whole. Beyond them lay a scattering of eccentric individuals and personal friends of the deposed king, such as Edward Nosworthy and William Penn.[77] The revival of Jacobitism in England is essentially the history of how these shattered remnants of the Jacobite regime persuaded other groups of malcontents to come into association with them.

Given the exigencies of power and the need for immediate action to remedy the grim situation in which it found itself early in 1689, the Williamite regime could not help but facilitate the process of Jacobite recrudescence. William, for example, could not turn a blind eye to the contumacy of a large part of the English clergy and episcopate. However unwilling he may have been to take drastic measures (and there is considerable evidence for his reluctance to do so), it was impossible for him to allow the Archbishop of Canterbury and other leading churchmen to continue in office after their conscience-stricken refusal to take the oaths of loyalty to him as king while James II still lived. Yet by stripping them of their clerical offices he created a major schism in the Church of England, for when around 400 clergymen who refused the oaths were excluded at the end of 1689 they were inevitably followed into the wilderness by a small but politically significant group of pious laity.[78] This stiff-necked group (both clergy and laity) was characterised as a whole by its principled refusal to swear oaths of loyalty to the new regime (in Latin: *jure*), and hence was known as the Nonjurors. Along with the Catholics, who of course had nowhere else to go for hope of alleviation of their plight, the Nonjurors were to become part of the bedrock of Jacobitism.

Another group the Williamite regime could hardly avoid alien-
ating was the political radicals who had welcomed William as a
liberator in 1688. William strove to conciliate conservative political
opinion almost from the moment he became king,[79] and in the
process naturally estranged many of his former allies. For the most
part, crypto-republicans like John Hampden and John Wildman
contented themselves with lambasting the iniquity of the new order
in print and in Parliament without seeking to overthrow it in favour
of the deposed James II.[80] A small, but significant, group of former
radicals, however, appear to have taken their opposition a stage
further and gone over to the Jacobites. Despairing of William III,
they turned to James II in the hope that if he was restored he
would be such a weak monarch, by virtue of his Catholicism and
debt to the Jacobites who had restored him, that they would be
able to extract major constitutional concessions.[81] Accomplished
conspirators like James Ferguson 'the Plotter' and polemicists like
Charlwood Lawton may not actually have had much more to offer
James II than their wits and their pens. But the Jacobite court was
convinced that it wielded great influence among the growing band
of Whigs disgruntled by the deracination, as they saw it, of Whig
principles by the Whig Junto Lords (the Earl of Orford (formerly
Admiral Russell), Lord Wharton, Lord Somers, Lord Halifax and
the Earl of Sunderland) who increasingly dominated the party
from 1690 onwards.[82] James II and his ministers accordingly valued
this group of Whig-Jacobites very highly, and if nothing else their
association with Jacobitism did allow it to present itself as a
much broader church than it was in reality. Other converts to
Jacobitism from within the Williamite regime, like the Earl (later
Duke) of Marlborough and the Duke of Shrewsbury, proved merely
transients, dabbling in Jacobitism for reinsurance purposes or while
they were out of office.[83] Nonetheless they too contributed to the
revival of Jacobitism over the generation following 1689 by keeping
up the Jacobite court's hopes of an imminent restoration – for why
else would such powerful men so humble themselves before the
king they had wronged?

The process of drawing other groups into support of the Jacobite
cause was considerably facilitated by the outcome of a power
struggle within the Jacobite movement.[84] Between 1689 and 1694
two factions fought a bruising battle for control of the Jacobite court
and its agenda in the event of a restoration: the 'Compounders' and

'Non-Compounders' (see pp. 30–1). In a sense their battle was over the soul of the Jacobite movement, for the appeal of governments-in-exile, oppositions, etc., has always centred on the things they promise to remedy or change in the event they come to power. The formal commitments made in such manifestos are thus made with a particular constituency in mind. Hence control over the draughting and content of such promissory agendas is of crucial importance to the political direction of exiled movements and opposition parties, which by their very nature tend to think a lot about the future. The Protestants' hard-won victory was thus of momentous consequence for the Jacobite cause. In essence it committed the Jacobites to a constitutional settlement in the event of a restoration that would, *de facto*, have been as emphatically Protestant as the developing Revolution settlement (see document 3).

Naturally enough, James II's co-religionists bitterly opposed his making commitments that threatened to leave them as badly off after a Jacobite restoration as before. And the royal family, mindful of the sacrifices and sufferings of its Catholic supporters as well its own intrinsic hostility to accepting the religious and political status quo, initially refused to contemplate making sweeping concessions to Protestant sensibilities. What eventually forced it to do so were the stark realities of the war. The political freedom to impose a settlement favourable to Catholics in Britain in the event of a restoration could only arise in the event of James reconquering his throne, and that could only happen with French assistance. By 1692 France was visibly struggling in the war and any hope of the massive, long-term military support that would have been necessary to maintain a Catholic regime had vanished. If the Jacobite court ever wanted to go home it was henceforth going to have to rely on its supporters in Britain.

Even in the 1690s the great majority of Jacobites still resident in Britain (outside Ireland) were Protestants. They correspondingly demanded concessions to their aspirations within the manifestos and declarations of its future intentions periodically issued by St Germain. James and the Catholic ministers who dominated the major offices of the exiled court, however, stubbornly refused to make the substantive changes the Protestants required. A complete impasse was only avoided by Louis XIV intervening on their behalf. Hard-headed as ever, the scourge of the Huguenots early in 1693 forced James to accept both a Secretary of State and a political manifesto from a Protestant faction centred on the Earl of Middleton. Just over a year later, this time in response to a direct appeal to him by some leading Protestants, Louis insisted that James dismiss his ablest Catholic minister, Melfort, leaving the field clear for Middleton, the Protestant Secretary of State, to steer the movement in a firmly Protestant direction.[85]

The immediate reaction in Britain to the sublimely moderate declaration issued by James II in April 1693 (see document 3) was mixed, but in the long term the Jacobite movement's decisive acceptance of a Protestant-dominated vision of a post-restoration settlement was momentous: it gave the Jacobite cause a future. Years later, as first-hand memories of James II's Catholic zeal faded and dissatisfaction with the Revolution settlement increased, it enabled the Jacobites to win support from a new generation of the politically discontented. There was, however, a price to pay. The new settlement effectively locked the Jacobites', 'pious, deeply Catholic kings . . . in a political settlement designed to accomodate the prejudices of their pious, deeply Protestant adherents.'[85] Such commitments naturally grated, though, by-and-large, James and his son glumly stuck with them. Nonetheless the tensions created by the exiled royal family's distaste for the agenda it was required to uphold laid the seeds for continuing religious conflict within the movement. And therein lay one of the major causes of the political paranoia that was to characterise the internal politics of the Jacobite movement for most of the eighteenth century.

The shift to a more Protestant-oriented ideological programme within Jacobitism preceded by only a few years a gathering crisis that unsettled many in Britain who had hitherto supported the Revolution settlement. A good many, if not most, of the Tories (traditionally the party of indefeasible hereditary right) who had accepted the Revolution and sworn allegiance in 1689 had salved their consciences over the plain fact of William and Mary's usurpation with the thought that it would not last long. William and Mary had been married since 1678 without producing any children. Their marriage was therefore unlikely to prove the seed of a new dynasty. Hence when William died either Mary or her sister Anne, both staunch Protestants in the direct line of descent from the Anglican martyr-king, Charles I, would succeed, and indefeasible hereditary right (i.e. strict patrilineal succession) would be restored, at least in the eyes of those Tories who could convince themselves the Old Pretender was a suppositious child.[86] Moreover, Anne's fecund marriage with Prince George of Denmark continued to offer hope that she would produce further Stuart heirs in the direct line.

Unfortunately for the Tories, such calculations ignored several unpalatable truths. The most difficult of these to overcome in the long term was that James Francis Edward Stuart, the Old Pretender, manifestly was the legitimate son and heir of James II. The right of the first born was his, and according to Anglican theology (the wellspring of Toryism) neither time nor statute law nor tradition could ameliorate the sin of usurpation implicit in the Revolution settlement. Next in importance were the grim statistics of Anne's fecundity. Of eighteen children born to her, only one, the Duke of Gloucester (born in 1689), had survived infancy, and he was a sickly child. When Anne's 'poor boy' died in 1700 it became brutally clear that the Protestant Stuart line was about to become extinct.[87] If the only surviving legitimate son of James II was barred from inheriting the throne, who was left? The answer was one calculated to make any High Anglican, xenophobic Tory blanch: the nearest Protestant heirs were the Lutheran, German Electors of Hanover.

As is often the case when people are aware of an unpalatable event in the offing that is, nevertheless, unlikely to materialise soon, the more conservative elements of the Tory political nation took the easy way out: they ignored the pending crisis. In 1701, when they were still recovering from the shock of Gloucester's death, Robert Harley managed to persuade the Tories to let a government-inspired Succession Act, spelling out the fact that the Hanoverian Guelfs were next in line of succession on Anne's death, pass the Commons.[88] Thereafter they appear to have simply tried not to think about it. Until 1710–11 Tories of all hues, but particularly the High Anglican wing of the party acted as if Queen Anne was immortal.[89] Only as her health visibly began to fail, from 1711 onwards, did they reluctantly begin to face the dilemma their ideology and the succession of the House of Hanover were going to place them in.

By then the problem had been compounded by the rise of High Toryism. A lay reflection of the High Church–Low Church rancour convulsing contemporary Anglicanism, this zealous, revanchist brand of Toryism was particularly strong among the backbench, or Country, Tories who dominated the Parliamentary Tory party.

Three subjects could be counted on to galvanise most High Tories: religious dissent, foreigners and the monarchy. Thus they were determined to uphold the Church of England by restricting or rolling back the religious toleration granted to Protestant dissenters in 1689, wished to exclude foreigners and foreign influence from British politics and society and displayed a ferocious loyalty to Queen Anne and the pre-Jacobite Stuart dynasty.[90] None of these preoccupations, of course, excluded loyalty to the Hanoverians. They did, however, make it increasingly difficult to contemplate their succession with equanimity. When all was said and done the Hanoverians were foreign religious dissenters, and their arrival would seal the extinction of a dynasty with which the High Tories were passionately emotionally identified. As a consequence, relations between the Hanoverians and the Tory party during Anne's reign tended to be wooden and formal at best. Individual Tories, such as William Bromley of Baginton and Sir Thomas Hanmer, could and did remain on cordial terms with the incoming dynasty, but the mass of the party appears to have been incapable of showing any enthusiasm for its future monarchs.[91]

This stood in stark contrast to the shameless toadying of the Whigs. By 1706 the Whigs had realised Queen Anne detested them (notwithstandng her fondness for individuals like Lord Cowper), and correspondingly devoted more and more effort to cultivating the reversionary interest.[92] After Harley's masterly political *putsch* levering them out of office in the summer of 1710, the Whigs devoted themselves still further to appearing as the guardians of the Protestant (Hanoverian) succession, even urging the German dynasty to invade England to secure its inheritance on one occasion.[93] The Hanoverians politely declined to get involved in such adventurism, but could not fail to be impressed by the contrast between the Whigs' zeal on their behalf and the Tories' coolness. As well, the future George I, who as Elector of Hanover was a loyal adherent of the imperial party in the Holy Roman Empire, naturally aligned himself with Emperor Charles VI when Charles declared his absolute opposition to the separate peace with France the Harley ministry began openly negotiating in 1711.[94] Because the Tories had become, by 1710, the peace party in contrast to the Whigs' determination to wage war *à l'outrance* against France, so the Guelfs' identification with a position the Tories assumed was pro-Whig further harmed their relations with Britain's prospective monarch.[95] And of course, once they were already estranged from the Hanoverians misinterpretations of the Guelfs' actions, and rumours about their secret hatred of the Tories as a whole, fed Tory neuroses about their succession to the throne. Relations between a German, Lutheran successor to the Stuarts and the rigidly Anglican, xenophobic and Stuart-worshipping radical fringe of the Tories were always liable to be fragile. Political events beyond the control of either party ensured they broke down.

The Jacobites were not especially well positioned to take advantage of the widening breach outlined above. After all, they could only offer a Frenchified Catholic as an alternative heir to Queen Anne. The Old Pretender's single advantage over his Hanoverian cousins was that he was a true Stuart, in the direct line of succession. Hence, despite the increasing dislike the Tories (especially the High Tories) were manifesting towards the Guelfs, they were not necessarily destined to become a Jacobite party. This is not to say that circumstances were not winning converts to Jacobitism within the Tory party. Between 1710 and 1714 such a substantial minority of Tory MPs and peers were showing Jacobite leanings that it became politically expedient for premier minister Harley (later Earl of Oxford) and his rival Henry St John (from 1712 Viscount Bolingbroke) both to cultivate connexions with the exiled Stuarts and even make secret promises of future (never present, before 1715) support.[96] What finally exasperated, and for a number of years irretrievably alienated, the Tories from the Hanoverians was the pronounced Whig bias they gave to the first ministry appointed after Queen Anne's death. A few dedicated pro-Hanoverian Tories were offered places and power. Most of them refused to go into office without the rest of their party.[97] As far as many Tories were concerned their 'exclusion' from government was a bitter vindication of all the predictions and warnings the Jacobites amongst them had been whispering for years. Church and state were apparently in the hands of a Whig king and his infidel creatures and urgently needed to be defended.[98] In such circumstances, where else did such English Tories have to go but the Pretender?

The rise of Jacobitism in Scotland, 1692–1715

Jacobitism in Scotland always operated from a firmer, and larger, base of support than its English counterpart, as may be seen from the two-year war in the Highlands waged by James's supporters there between 1689 and 1691. Yet the defeat of James's adherents in a straight fight conversely acted to diminish their influence and restrain their enthusiasm for some time after the clans' submission to the government early in 1692.[99] What revived the Jacobite cause in Scotland was its association with opposition to the Williamite regime. Because it was well known to be the mortal enemy of the established order, Jacobitism naturally drew to itself those elements in Scottish society and politics who were disgusted with the status quo.

There was, moreover, much to be disgusted at. Whereas a key feature of the Revolution settlement in England was the enactment of a religious toleration covering virtually all Protestants, the principal thrust of its Scottish analogue was to reimpose a Presbyterian regime on the Kirk and deny religious toleration to Episcopalian Protestants.[100] It is true that many Episcopalian Scots (including the majority of the bishops) were already committed to the Jacobite cause by the time the legislation was passed, yet others were at least neutral towards the Williamite regime before it took up the banner of strict Presbyterianism, and could have formed the nucleus of a pro-Revolution episcopalian church.[101] Instead, the triumphal Presbyterianism of the Kirk settlement bulldozed through by the Earl of Crawford and the Presbyterian party in 1689–90, swiftly eliminated Episcopalian support for a moderate response to the new order. The expulsions of Episcopalian clergymen from their parishes and the imposition of the machinery of Presbyterian discipline on hostile, pro-Episcopalian congregations in the decade following reinforced the Episcopalians' inherent inclination to support the Jacobite cause.[102] By 1700 the Episcopalian clergy and hierarchy – i.e. the spiritual mentors of *at least* 20 per cent of the Scottish population – were so imbued with bitter Jacobitism that it would take the best part of a century of defeats to persuade them to reconsider their commitment to the cause of the exiled Stuarts.

The new regime was further compromised in the eyes of a large part of the Scottish political nation by its association with a series of horrors and disasters over which, in reality, it had very little control. The first and most notorious of these was the infamous massacre of the Macdonalds at Glencoe in 1692. The government's responsibility for what occurred there was actually incidental. Sir

John Dalrymple of Stair, who hated popery and papist clansmen with a vengeance, issued an order for the chastisement of the Macdonalds of Glencoe with 'Fire and Sword' after they apparently refused to submit to the government along with the other clans. By the time his order arrived the Macdonalds of Glencoe, who had actually been dragging their feet about formally submitting so as to score points against their Highland neighbours, had belatedly surrendered. Dalrymple's orders, however, were issued to Robert Campbell of Glenlyon and a force of Campbell levies who had their own scores to settle with their troublesome neighbours, which they duly did on the night of 13 February 1692.[103] Nonetheless, it was the government which was blamed when news of the massacre became public, Parliamentary inquiries were inaugurated by opponents of the regime and the participants scrambled to exculpate themselves.[104]

Even as news of the Glencoe massacre was being publicised by Sir James Montgomerie of Skelmorlie in his pamphlet, *Great Britain's Just Complaint* in September 1692, Scotland was on the verge of entering the period later known as 'King William's seven ill years'. The harvest failed in Scotland for two years running between 1696 and 1698, and, as was inevitable in a pious, Bible-reading society, the famine which ensued was interpreted in the light of similar events in the Old Testament, the analogy in this case being drawn with the way God had smitten Egypt in the time of Moses.[105] It is interesting that the Pharaonic analogy became the most popular. Pharaoh was the archetype of the unjust ruler, and the metaphor thus implies a great deal about subsequent Scots opinion of William III. Obviously the Scottish government could not be held responsible for the famine, which may have killed or driven into exile as much as one-third of Scotland's population. In an age accustomed to finding visible signs of God's grace (or the lack of it) in both individuals and institutions, however, governments which presided over natural disasters like famines were often regarded as tainted. Hence the Williamite regime, and by implication the Revolution, became associated in the minds of many Scots with divine wrath – a connexion which could not fail to redound to the advantage of the Jacobites.

To round off a decade marked by civil war, massacre and famine, Scotland entered into a disastrous colonial adventure in the late 1690s. Once again, the Darien disaster, in which

Scots investors from every social stratum sank all they could into a futile attempt to found a trading colony on the isthmus of Darien in Spanish America, cannot fairly be ascribed to anything the government did. It had more in common with mass speculative fever, like that experienced in England during the South Sea Bubble, than government policy. Nonetheless, when the colony failed the Williamite administration in Scotland, the king and the English Parliament were all blamed for not having supported the venture with arms and money.[106] It is perhaps a measure of the weakness of the Williamite regime in Scotland that it could not prevent the speculative fever that fuelled the Darien adventure building up in the first place, and was left to pick up the pieces by William III and the English Parliament after the disaster ran its course.[107]

The weakness of the Williamite regime in Scotland underlay all the developments outlined above. It stemmed partly from the Scottish state's fiscal bankruptcy in the face of the demands of the Highland war, which necessitated accepting substantial subsidies and help from England, and partly from the invidious position Scotland's governing elite were placed in by William's lack of interest in Scottish affairs. Under the later Stuarts Scottish affairs had been run by virtual satraps like the Duke of Lauderdale and the Drummond brothers, who were allowed to dispense patronage and use their authority in any way that kept the country quiet and the crown firmly in control. William, out of ignorance or indifference, at first ignored this precedent and tried to run Scotland, like England, through coalitions in which all shades of opinion within the 'Revolution interest' were reflected. The Scots magnates, however, were unaware that the rules had changed and therefore dedicated themselves to undermining their colleagues and building up a dominant position within the administration. They did so by violently factional politics within the Scots Parliament, and by busily hunting up English allies at court and at Westminster. When added to the new freedom to dispute government policy and decisions created in the Scottish Parliament by the abolition in 1689 of the official steering committee that had effectively checked it for most of the century (the Lords of the Articles), these disputes among the magnates produced a veritable inclination toward political chaos.[108]

For in the Scottish Parliament from 1689 onwards a permanent, radical core of opposition developed. Centred on ostentatious 'patriots' like Sir James Montgomery of Skelmorlie and Andrew Fletcher of Saltoun, it provided a fixed base of opposition to the administration of the day. On one level this meant that disgruntled magnates like Argyll, Atholl and the Duke of Hamilton could always find a body of allies outside the government when they did one of their periodic shuttles between government and opposition.[109] More fundamentally, the rise of a permanent chorus of ideological, patriotic opposition acted to throw the self-interest and corruption of Scotland's rulers into a worse light than ever. As well, that fixed core of opposition inevitably represented a potential recruiting ground for the inveterate opponents of the Williamite regime and all its works: the Jacobites. It is instructive to note that as early as 1690 some members of the radical 'Club' opponents of the ministry in the Scottish Parliament, in particular Montgomery of Skelmorlie, were already dallying with the Jacobites and discussing plans for a joint uprising.[110] As the grim events of the 1690s unfolded and the Williamite regime became enmired in the Glencoe massacre, the famine and the Darien disaster, more and more of the Scots political nation began to listen to the thunderous denunciations emanating from the Country opposition. Even William's grudging acceptance of the need to appoint a neo-satrap in 1698 (the Duke of Queensberry) could not check the process. Between the intractably factious magnates and their clients, and the burgeoning Country party with its Jacobite tendencies, there was an increasing prospect that Scotland would soon prove to be ungovernable from London, i.e. the Scottish Parliament would start overriding policy and decisions stemming from Westminster.

The Duke of Queensberry and the Revolution interest in Scotland were considerably hampered in their efforts to hold off this dire possibility by the insensitivity of William and his ministers to the rising tide of patriotic feeling in Scotland. In 1701 the English Parliament, at the ministry's behest, passed the Act of Settlement designating the House of Hanover the heirs to William III and Princess Anne in both kingdoms. At no point was the Scottish Parliament or political nation consulted about a measure that directly affected them. While Scottish outrage at this slight was gathering steam the Scottish Parliament of 1689 met for the last time. Queensberry and his masters at Westminster prolonged its existence for as long as possible to avoid facing the electorate, but a taxpayers' strike finally forced a general election in 1703 in which the political nation vented its spleen by returning crypto-Jacobites in such numbers they were able to coalesce into a distinct party in their own right: the Cavaliers. And in association with their Whiggish allies in the Country party and disgruntled magnates like the Duke of Hamilton, they were able to push through the Act Anent Peace and War in 1703 and the Act of Security in 1704.[111] The Act Anent Peace and War denied control of Scotland's foreign policy to any Westminster-based government after the death of Queen Anne. The Act of Security flatly stated that unless Scotland's grievances were satisfactorily redressed during Anne's lifetime, whoever inherited the English throne would be ineligible to succeed her in Scotland. The northern kingdom was threatening to escape the embraces of its southern neighbour – a threat no English politician could ignore.

The response of the Marlborough–Godolphin ministry was accordingly prompt. The ministry in Scotland was bolstered up with subsidies and other forms of patronage and the English Parliament was persuaded to pass the Aliens Act. This would have treated the Scots on a par with other foreigners with respect to trade and civil rights.[112] It constituted the stick in negotiations for a union of the two kingdoms that were set in train at the same time. The treaty of Union that emerged from the Anglo-Scottish negotiations (with a carefully selected, almost entirely pro-Union membership in both delegations) was the carrot. It was a masterpiece of douceurs and special deals designed to buy off or weaken powerful interest groups that might have been opposed to a union. The Presbyterian clergy were bought off with a separate church settlement for Scotland that left the Kirk distinct from the Church of England and under their control. The lawyers were bought off by a clause preserving Scotland's separate legal system. The Darien Company's creditors were promised repayment based on the repatriation to Scotland of taxation levied on the united kingdoms to service the English national debt, and so on.[113] It was all designed to achieve one end: the passage through the Scots Parliament of an incorporating union, i.e. a fusion of Scotland and England's representative institutions. Since any clauses guaranteeing Scotland's constitutional rights were carefully excluded from the final treaty, this was bound to leave Scotland at the mercy of the much larger English representation envisaged in the united Parliament.

The Jacobites and patriots in the Scottish Parliament quickly recognised the threat the treaty posed and raised a furore inside and outside the House that at several points threatened to block the passage of the Act of Union. They were considerably helped by the manifest anger of the Scottish political nation and, indeed, the nation at large at the prospect of their representatives voting away their nationhood. Passage of the treaty of Union into law was correspondingly marked by outbursts of savage rioting and threatened uprisings. Nonetheless, by making a great many private promises of future patronage and favour to politicians like the Earl of Mar and Hamilton, bombarding Scottish MPs and peers with pro-Union propaganda (courtesy of that well-known government hack, Daniel Defoe) and by carefully greasing the wheels of power with a secret subvention of £20,000 to Queensberry to pay 'arrears' of pensions and salaries, the government at Westminster eventually secured the passage of the Act of Union on 16 January 1707.[114]

This was far from being the end of the affair. While the Act of Union was passing the Scots Parliament troops were guarding the building to prevent incensed mobs invading it. Formal covenants and declarations against the Union were taken up in the north and west of Scotland.[115] None of these disorganised manifestations of public hostility towards the Union led to anything in its immediate aftermath, but, as we have already seen, the Jacobites were able to use the visible anger of the Scottish people to convince the French that it was worthwhile invading Scotland. The invasion failed of course, yet it seems reasonable to conjecture that had the French landed with the Old Pretender at their head promising to dissolve the Union, they would have attracted a good deal of popular support.

Over the next seven years the behaviour of the English majority in the new British Parliament toward Scots affairs and concerns, moreover, did nothing to conciliate those sections of Scottish opinion that were hostile to the Union. A draconian Treason Act that rode roughshod over Scottish legal practice was enacted in 1708. In 1711, in a piece of manifestly chauvinist political chicanery, those holding Scots peerages (and their heirs ever after) at the time of the Union were barred from sitting in the Lords as hereditary British peers.[116] To the disgust of the Scottish Kirk, in 1712 English bishops and peers calmly legislated a religious toleration for Scots Episcopalian dissenters, the restoration of lay patronage of ecclesiastical livings and the reinstitution of Christmas holidays in Scotland – all in complete defiance of the spirit of the Union.[117] In 1713, when Scotland was for the first time subjected to English levels of taxation on a staple crop (malt) – again in defiance of the letter of the Union treaty – the Scots representatives in Parliament moved for a dissolution of the association.[118] They were, of course, defeated by the English majority, whose attitude is well summarised in the words of a prominent English MP, who stated that though he, 'was not very fond of the Union in all respects . . .since there were some advantages to England from it, and that they had catcht hold of Scotland, they wou'd keep her fast'.[119] The net effect was that by the time of the Hanoverian succession in 1714 there was a pervasive disillusion with the Union and much that stemmed from it. This feeling was expressed in a petitioning movement over the winter of 1714–15 calling on the new dynasty, now it was safely esconced in power, to allow its dissolution. Despite the best endeavours of the Whig administration in Scotland to suppress such an overt statement of hostility towards the new order, it garnered a good deal of support.[120] Correspondingly, the petition's rejection by George I and his Whig ministers seemed to many Scots finally to indicate the exhaustion of all constitutional means for the redress of Scotland's grievances.

The 1715 rebellion

It will by now be obvious that the roots of the '15 were deep ones in both Scotland and England. This accords with the importance of the rising. The '15 was potentially the most serious Jacobite rising of the eighteenth century. There is a deep irony in this, as it was an incredibly botched job on the part of the Jacobites. Yet it still shook the foundations of the Whig regime in the British Isles. The remainder of this chapter is concerned with tracing the outbreak and course of the rebellion, and, perhaps most importantly of all, suggesting why it failed.

Though it should not have done so, the death of Queen Anne caught the Jacobites unprepared. In the last months of her life the Old Pretender and his advisers at St Germain had slowly begun to hearken to the repeated warnings from their adherents

73

in Britain not to trust either Oxford or Bolingbroke, both of whom were ostensibly 'negotiating' the terms of a restoration with the Jacobite court.[121] There had not been enough time, however, to build up a military alternative to a Parliamentary restoration. The French secretly promised two ships to convey the Old Pretender to England or Scotland, but absolutely refused to supply him with any troops lest it provoke renewed hostilities against France by the Grand Alliance.[122] The Jacobites in Britain were also unenthusiastic about the prospect of rebelling without a body of professional troops in support, and, caught between their uncertainty and France's unwillingness to get openly involved, the Old Pretender was unable to do anything more than issue a formal protest when George I peacefully succeeded to the throne.[123]

George I's determination, however, to secure his dynasty's hold on Britain as rapidly as possible, effectively locked him into relying on the Whigs for support and advice. He was in too much of a hurry to waste time wooing the Tories. As a result, the legacy of distrust built up between the Tories and the Guelfs in the final years of Queen Anne now came home to roost with a vengeance. A tiny handful of resolutely pro-Hanoverian Tories (so pro-Hanoverian they had opposed the Oxford ministry because of its lukewarmness on the issue) were admitted to office. The rest of George I's first ministry was overwhelmingly Whig. In addition, officeholders appointed under the previous, Tory, regime were purged on a large scale and replaced by their Whig rivals.[124] In many respects this was the normal currency of politics. But in the charged atmosphere of distrust and apprehension that prevailed throughout the winter of 1714–15 many Tories put a far more sinister interpretation on what was going on. It is plainly the case that the Church of England was in no more danger under the first Hanoverians than it had been under Queen Anne. Yet the Tories entered the 1715 general election campaign with a manifesto of grievances and dire warnings centred on that most emotive of issues. Its presence was not just political; it was symptomatic of a genuine fear among the Tories that their beloved church was about to fall into the hand of infidels and thieves.[125] Confirmation of all their neuroses seemed to be forthcoming in the spring of 1715 when, having won a thumping victory (in terms of seats, but *not* votes[126]) in the general election, the Whigs opened impeachment proceedings against the leaders of the Tory party, Oxford, Bolingbroke, the Earl of Strafford and the Duke of Ormond, for their part in the secret peace negotiations with France leading to the Peace of Utrecht. Oxford and Strafford brazened it out, but Bolingbroke and Ormond fled to France in panic (where they both subsequently joined the Old Pretender).[127] It was the final straw. Out of the fear the Whigs' proceedings provoked among the Tories came the support for a rising in England without which the Jacobites could never have got the '15 off the ground.

The unfortunate (from the Jacobite standpoint) corollary of the shift of opinion among a large section of England's Tories in favour of a recourse to arms in 1715 was the injection of a great deal of *naiveté* into Jacobite planning there. The hard core Jacobites could not fail by 1715 to be aware of most of the difficulties conspiracies were bound to run into in this age of easily intercepted communications.[128] The Tories were much less prepared for what was likely to ensue when the government caught wind of their plans. In this context it is instructive to note that plebeian Tories-cum-Jacobites in England expressed themselves far more vociferously against the Hanoverian regime in rioting throughout the winter of 1714–15, reaching a crescendo in the spring and early summer, than their Scottish counterparts.[129] Yet when the time for action came the social superiors of the mobs proclaiming 'King James III' or bawling 'No Cuckold! No Hanover!' in streets and market-squares across the Midlands and south of England were paralysed with fear and indecision. When the Earl of Mar realised the government was on to the conspiracy he smartly absconded to the Highlands and raised the standard of rebellion.[130] His English fellow-conspirator Sir William Wyndham by contrast wandered disconsolately around the south-west in disguise before surrendering himself to the authorities.[131] Correspondingly, the English half of the '15 went off like a damp squib. The government responded to the wave of Tory/Jacobite rioting by bending all its efforts to find out if anything more serious than plebeian discontent underlay the phenomenon. Once it began looking, of course it soon learnt what was going on and ordered the arrest of the major actors.[132] Lord Lansdown was swept up in August, Wyndham was forced to flee soon after, and all that remained were second-rankers afraid to mark themselves out by taking decisive action. Hence on the day appointed for the rising in the south-west a large number of Tory gentry turned up for a 'race-meeting' at Bath, milled around a little and then, advised by a letter from Wyndham (still in hiding) that all was lost, quietly departed homewards.[133]

Only in the north of England did the English Jacobites manage to get the planned insurrection off the ground, and then only with considerable help from their Scottish neighbours over the nearby border. The MP Thomas Forster and the Catholic Earl of Derwentwater both fled into the Northumberland hills in September 1715 on receiving news that they were about to be arrested. There they gathered a small force of their more courageous friends and servants and proclaimed the Old Pretender. Apparently at a loss what to do next, they halfheartedly tried to take Newcastle by surprise, and on being repulsed (or rather, deterred), proceeded to wander up and down the borders picking up recruits and waiting for something to happen. They were rescued from their chronic state of indecision by the arrival on the border of a party of Scots lowland rebels under Viscount Kenmuir and the Earl of Carnwath, and a considerably larger force of Highlanders under the command of Brigadier-General William Mackintosh of Borlum. These reinforcements provided the little army with the steel to march south and it duly advanced as far as Preston before it was cornered by two small government forces under Generals Wills and Carpenter. Borlum and his Highlanders efficiently barricaded the town and they and their English Jacobite peers gave a reasonably good account of themselves, repulsing at least two attacks with loss. At that point, however, Forster and Derwentwater's nerve seems to have been broken by the horror and destruction they were witnessing and they both insisted on surrendering – much to the surprise of the besiegers and the fury of the Scots.[134]

As will by now be appreciated from the foregoing account of events in England, the mainstay of the '15 had to be Scotland. Essentially the distinction between the rising in the two countries lay in the greater determination of the Scots rebels and the ambivalence, even friendly neutrality, of much of the Scottish population. Not many Scots were willing to volunteer to fight for the government and the Union in 1715. The disparity between the native forces raised by both sides in Scotland during the opening stages of the rebellion is correspondingly striking. Taking into account the turnout of potential rebels, plus the turnover in their ranks as some men drifted home while others joined up, something in the region of 20,000 Scots may have appeared (however briefly) in arms for the Jacobite cause. Conversely, by the same criteria, probably less than 7,000 joined the government's forces. This would translate statistically as about 8 per cent of the adult male Scots population turning out for King James as compared with about 2.5 per cent for King George.[135] By any standards this was a very serious uprising in which the rebels enjoyed far more support than the government.

In order to win, however, the promising levels of support the Jacobites enjoyed had to be translated into captured cities and victories on the battlefield. And herein lay the failure of the revolt in Scotland and consequently throughout the British Isles. The organiser and leader of the rebellion in Scotland was the Earl of Mar. A former pro-Unionist and Secretary of State for Scotland in Queen Anne's last ministry, as we have seen, he appears to have been driven to desperation by the prospect of losing all hope, for the foreseeable future anyway, of regaining the government office so necessary to maintain his local power and self-esteem. Fleeing from London in August just in time to evade arrest for complicity in the Jacobite plotting that had been underway since the spring of 1715, he withdrew into the Highlands and there summoned the clan chieftains and north-eastern Episcopalian notables to rise for King James.[136] This was the limit of his military expertise. He had no idea how to run an army, still less how to conduct a military campaign. Hence the advances the rebels made and the successes they scored in September and October in northern and western Scotland, such as the Master of Sinclair's Burntisland raid, were almost entirely due to the dash and initiative of his subordinates.[137] Instead of attacking the tiny government garrison in Scotland as soon as he had the opportunity, Mar camped at Perth and awaited French reinforcement.

He appears to have been hoping that the Duke of Berwick, James II's illegitimate son and a marshal of France, would arrive and take over. Berwick (a naturalised Frenchman), had, however, been refused permission to join the rebellion by Louis XIV, and refused to gamble everything he had on such a risky venture – despite the desperate and increasingly angry remonstrations of the Old Pretender.[138] Consequently the Duke of Argyll was able to scrape together a force of 1,500 regular troops and supplement them with a further 1,500 volunteers before Mar reluctantly agreed to advance southwards from Perth. The two armies duly encountered each other at Sherrifmuir on 13 November in an indecisive clash that glaringly reveals the nature of the Jacobite failure in the '15. Argyll drew up his 3,000 men in two wings: the professional soldiers on his right, the Whig volunteers on his left. Mar arranged his roughly 10,000 men in one long line according to the nuances of clan rivalries, then charged. Both sides' left wing was routed, but as a result Argyll was left in the more precarious position: midway through the battle he was left with little more than 1,000 men to face the victorious regiments of the right of the Jacobite line, who probably numbered something around 5,000. Mar, who had led the Jacobite charge, at that moment held the fate of the rebellion in his hand. While nothing is certain in history, and still less in war, it seems highly likely that had Mar ordered a renewed onslaught against Argyll's beleaguered professionals, he would have overwhelmed them. Instead of attacking, however, he withdrew from the field claiming victory – leaving Argyll's army battered but intact.[139]

The indecisive battle at Sherrifmuir proved the death-knell of the rebellion. Mar retired to Perth and obdurately refused to advance again. His army, disillusioned with him and increasingly apprehensive about its future, began to melt away. Meanwhile Argyll rallied his forces, then steadily built up a formidable army with reinforcements from England and the Netherlands. The Old Pretender's arrival in Scotland on 22 December might have rallied the dispirited Jacobite army, had he been accompanied by Berwick or possessed more military talent himself, but it was not to be. James deferred to Mar from the start and the military situation correspondingly continued to deteriorate. By February 1716 it was clear that Argyll had more than sufficient forces to crush the Jacobites if they dared to offer battle. James and Mar accordingly abandoned the army to Major-General Alexander Gordon of Auchintoul and took ship to France. Gordon thereupon retired to the Highlands and ordered what was left of the army to disperse.[140] Apart from the inevitable spate of exemplary executions of selected Jacobite prisoners, the '15 was over, and with it the first stage of development of the Jacobite movement.

Notes

1 For the rise of the new model British state see: J. Brewer, *The Sinews of Power, War, Money and the English State, 1688–1793*, New York, 1989.

2 H. Horwitz, *Parliament, Policy and Politics in the Reign of William III*, Manchester, 1977, p. 20.

3 G. Symcox, 'Louis XIV and the outbreak of the Nine Years War', in R. Hatton, ed., *Louis XIV and Europe*, 1976, pp. 196–204; Childs, *Nine Years War*, p. 101.

4 P. W. J. Riley, *King William and the Scottish Politicians*, Edinburgh, 1979, pp. 11–15.

5 Hopkins, *Glencoe*, pp. 125–9, 132.

6 J. G. Simms, *Jacobite Ireland 1685–91*, 1969, pp. 48–52.

7 J. T. Gilbert, ed., *A Jacobite Narrative of the War in Ireland, 1688–1691*, Shannon, repr. 1971, p. 47.

8 T. W. Moody, F. X. Martin and F. J. Byrne, eds *A New History of Ireland, III: Early Modern Ireland 1534–1691*, Oxford, 1976, p. 491; Simms, *Jacobite Ireland*, pp. 77–93 *passim*.

9 Ibid., p. 88.

10 Hopkins, *Glencoe*, p. 143.

11 J. Childs, *The British Army of William III, 1689–1702*, Manchester, 1987, pp. 4–30.

12 Horwitz, *Parliament*, pp. 26–30, 32–5.

13 Hopkins, *Glencoe*, pp. 142–60.

14 Ibid., pp. 178–212 *passim*.

15 Riley, *King William*, pp. 22–39.

16 Hopkins, *Glencoe*, pp. 215–18.

17 Ibid., pp. 232–79, 296–7, 316–17.

18 See, for example, the 'Irish Alarms' of December 1688, analysed in G. H. Jones, 'The Irish fright of 1688: real violence and imagined massacre', *Bulletin of the Institute of Historical Research*, LV, 1982, pp. 148–53.

19 Simms, *Jacobite Ireland*, pp. 57, 95–100.

20 P. Aubrey, *The Defeat of James Stuart's Armada 1692*, Leicester, 1979, p. 35.

21 Simms, *Jacobite Ireland*, pp. 109–13, 117–18.

22 Ibid., pp. 120–30.

23 Ibid., pp. 136–7.

24 J. Hogan, ed., *Negociations de M. Le Comte D'Avaux en Irlande 1689–90*, Irish Manuscripts Commission, Dublin, 1934, pp. 78, 140, 334; *Jacobite Narrative*, pp. 83, 90.

25 Childs, *Nine Years War*, pp. 42, 87.

26 *Life of James II*, II, pp. 636–8.

27 C. O'Kelly, 'Macariae excidium or the destruction of Cyprus', in T. C. Croker, ed., *Narratives Illustrative of the Contests in Ireland in 1641 and 1690, Camden Society*, XIV, 1841, pp. 34, 35, 63, 64.

28 Ibid., p. 37; *Jacobite Narrative*, pp. 47–54, 91; *Negociations*, pp. 84, 159, 183, 184–5.

29 'Macariae excidium', pp. 58–9.

30 Miller, *James II*, 224–5.

31 Simms, *Jacobite Ireland*, pp. 141–52.

32 *Eighteenth-Century Ireland*, p. 397; *Early Modern Ireland*, p. 498.

33 Simms, *Jacobite Ireland*, pp. 155–60.

34 Ibid., pp. 163–72.

35 D. Chandler, *Marlborough as Military Commander*, 2nd edn, 1979, pp. 37–42.

36 Simms, *Jacobite Ireland*, 202–12.

37 Ibid., pp. 216–36, 243–58.

38 Brewer, *Sinews of Power*, pp. 29–31, 34–5, 39–40, 46, 88–9, 91–8, 101–4, 114, 119.

39 Childs, *Nine Years War*, p. 1.

40 D. Hayton, 'The Country interest and the party system', in C. Jones, ed., *Party and Management in Parliament, 1660–1784*, Leicester, 1984, pp. 59–60; National Library of Wales, Aberystwyth, Ottley MS 2448: Thomas Strangways to Lieutenant Ottley (c. April 1712).

41 Holmes, *British Politics*, pp. 97–101; *Trial of Dr Sacheverell*, pp. 35–41.

42 B. P. Lenman and J. S. Gibson, *The Jacobite Threat: England, Scotland, Ireland, France. A Source Book*, Edinburgh, 1990, pp. 13–15.

43 Ferguson, *Scotland's Relations with England*, pp. 170–4.

44 D. Szechi and D. Hayton, 'John Bull's other kingdoms: the government of Scotland and Ireland', in C. Jones, ed., *Britain in the First Age of Party 1680–1750. Essays Presented to Geoffrey Holmes*, 1987, pp. 265–8.

45 *Eighteenth-Century Ireland*, pp. 16–21, 26.

46 Szechi and Hayton, 'John Bull's other kingdoms', pp. 68–70.

47 *Eighteenth-Century Ireland*, pp. 406–7.

48 Ibid., pp. 630–9.

49 Childs, *Nine Years War*, pp. 5, 26.

50 Brewer, *Sinews of Power*, pp. 33–7.

51 Aubrey, *Defeat of James Stuart's Armada*, pp. 29–133.

52 G. Symcox, *The Crisis of French Naval Power, 1688–97*, 1974.

53 Childs, *Nine Years War*, pp. 178–209, 215–45 esp. 234–60; *Army of William III*, pp. 4–30.

54 Childs, *Nine Years War*, pp. 133–4, 214, 246, 250, 264; Cf. F. Bluche, *Louis XIV*, transl. M. Greengrass, New York, 1990, pp. 438–41.

55 Childs, *Nine Years War*, p. 341.

56 Baxter, *William III*, p. 305.

57 C. Duffy, *The Military Experience in the Age of Reason*, 1987, pp. 197–8, 200–19, 233–6, 239–54.

58 See for example: Hopkins, *Glencoe*, 208–9, 219–21; HMC, Stuart, I, p. 268: Duke of Berwick to the Old Pretender, 26 June 1713 ns.

59 P. Hopkins, 'Sham plots and real plots in the 1690s', in Cruikshanks, *Ideology and Conspiracy*, 89–102; cf. Monod, *Jacobitism*, pp. 309–14.

60 Jones, *Main Stream*, pp. 23–4.

61 *Memoirs of Thomas, Earl of Ailesbury. Written by himself*, ed. E. Buckley, Roxburghe Club, 1890, I, p. 323.

62 Childs, *Army of William III*, p. 175.

63 Jones, *Main Stream*, p. 45.

64 *Life of James II*, II, pp. 538–43.

65 Jones, *Main Stream*, pp. 47–8; Monod, *Jacobitism*, pp. 99–100.

66 Chandler, *Marlborough*, pp. 151–83.

67 *Correspondence of Colonel N. Hooke, passim*.

68 J. S. Gibson, *Playing the Scottish Card. The Franco-Jacobite Invasion of 1708*, Edinburgh, 1988, pp. 98–9.

69 M. Haile, *James Francis Edward. The Old Chevalier*, 1907, pp. 87–8.

70 Gibson, *Scottish Card*, pp. 117–29, 139–45.

71 Monod, *Jacobitism*, pp. 28–44, 47–69.

72 The consequences of detection could, however, be dire. Cf. the fate of John Matthews (Monod, *Jacobitism*, p. 40) and George Flint (P. B. Hyland, 'Liberty and libel: government and the press during the succession crisis in Britain, 1712–16', *English Historical Review*, CI, 1986, pp. 863–88).

73 M. Harris, 'Print and politics in the age of Walpole', in J. Black, ed., *Britain in the Age of Walpole*, 1984, pp. 197–202.

74 See for example, D. Szechi, *Jacobitism and Tory Politics 1710–14*, Edinburgh, 1984, *passim*.

75 Hence the prominence of Jacobites among backbench Tory organisations such as the October Club, for which see: H. T. Dickinson, 'The October Club', *Huntington Library Quarterly*, XXXIII, 1969–70, pp. 155–74, and Szechi, *Jacobitism and Tory Politics*, pp. 75–84.

76 Jones, 'Irish fright'; A. Browning, ed., *Memoirs of Sir John Reresby*, Glasgow, 1936, pp. 521–30.

77 B. D. Henning, ed., *The House of Commons 1660–1690*, 3 vols., 1983, III, pp. 165–6; Jones, *Main Stream*, pp. 17, 20.

78 Monod, *Jacobitism*, 139, 142–3.

79 Horwitz, *Parliament*, pp. 17–19.

80 M. Goldie, 'The roots of true Whiggism 1688–94', *History of Political Thought*, I, 1980, pp. 195–236.

81 Monod, *Jacobitism*, pp. 23–7.

82 Plumb, *Political Stability*, pp. 135–9.

83 D. H. Somerville, *King of Hearts. Charles Talbot, Duke of Shrewsbury*, 1962, pp. 76–80; D. Szechi, 'The Duke of Shrewsbury's contacts with the Jacobites in 1713', *Bulletin of the Institute of Historical Research*, LVI, 1983, pp. 229–32.

84 What follows below on this subject is derived from my article 'Revolution Settlement', which should be consulted for a closer analysis of these events. For a different interpretation see: Monod, 'Jacobitism and Country principles', pp. 289–310.

85 Ibid., p. 628.

86 Dickinson, *Liberty and Property*, pp. 37–40.

87 Gregg, *Queen Anne*, pp. 120–2.

88 B. W. Hill, *Robert Harley. Speaker, Secretary of State and Premier Minister*, 1988, p. 66.

89 Holmes, *British Politics*, p. 90, and see for example, *Lockhart Papers*, I, pp. 468–9.

90 J. P. Kenyon, *Revolution Principles. The Politics of Party 1689–1720*, 1977, pp. 61–101; Holmes, *British Politics*, pp. 64–9.

91 Ibid., pp. 87–95; Sedgwick, *House of Commons*, I, p. 493, II, p. 107.

92 Holmes, *British Politics*, p. 83; Gregg, *Queen Anne*, p. 219; *Original Papers*, II, pp. 33–5, 94, 139, 183, 482, 596–8.

93 E. Gregg, 'Marlborough in exile, 1712–1714', *Historical Journal*, XV, 1972, p. 599.

94 Hatton, *George I*, pp. 105–6.

95 Holmes, *British Politics*, pp. 75–80.

96 Szechi, *Jacobitism and Tory Politics*, pp. 182–91, 200–3.

97 Colley, *In Defiance*, pp. 177–82.

98 F. Atterbury, *English Advice To the Freeholders of England*, 1714, in *A Third Collection of Scarce and Valuable Tracts*, 4 vols., 1751, IV, pp. 359–78.

99 *Original Papers*, II, pp. 529–30: Middleton to Sir William Bruce, 23 December 1695 ns.

100 Riley, *King William*, pp. 35–7.

101 Lenman, *Jacobite Risings*, p. 55; *Lockhart Papers*, I, pp. 84–5.

102 Lenman, *Jacobite Risings*, pp. 56–68.

103 Hopkins, *Glencoe*, chapter 10.

104 Ibid., chapter 12.

105 R. Mitchison, *Lordship to Patronage. Scotland 1603–145*, 1983, pp. 108–10.

106 J. Prebble, *The Darien Disaster*, 1968.

107 Riley, *King William*, pp. 132–3.

108 Szechi and Hayton, 'John Bull's other kingdoms', pp. 243–51.

109 Ibid., pp. 250–2.

110 Hopkins, *Glencoe*, pp. 208–9.

111 Ferguson, *Scotland's Relations*, pp. 197–201, 202–4, 208–12, 218–20.

112 Ibid., pp. 222–3.

113 Lenman, *Jacobite Risings*, pp. 83–6.

114 Ferguson, *Scotland's Relations*, pp. 238–53, 266–9.

115 *Lockhart Papers*, I, pp. 194–200.

116 G. S. Holmes, 'The Hamilton affair of 1711–12: a crisis in Anglo-Scottish relations', *English Historical Review*, LXXVII, 1962, pp. 257–82.

117 D. Szechi, 'The politics of 'persecution': Scots Episcopalian toleration and the Harley ministry', in W. J. Sheils, ed., *Toleration and Persecution, Studies in Church History*, XXI, 1984, pp. 275–89.

118 Szechi, *Jacobitism and Tory Politics*, pp. 125, 130–5. For a different emphasis, see G. S. Holmes and C. Jones, 'Trade, the Scots and the parliamentary crisis of 1713', *Parliamentary History*, I, 1982, pp. 47–77.

119 *Lockhart Papers*, I, p. 427.

120 National Library of Scotland, Acc. 7124, Lockhart of Lee and Carnwath estate papers: open letter from the freeholders of Fife, 5 October 1714; Wodrow Letters VIII, ep. 156, 160–5; IX, esp. 4–5, 8, 12, 18.

121 Szechi, *Jacobitism and Tory Politics*, pp. 93–5, 101–3, 124–6, 157–61, 182–91.

122 Ibid., p. 189.

123 Carte MS 180, f. 1: 29 August 1714 ns.

124 Plumb, *Political Stability*, pp. 159–64.

125 Bennett, *Tory Crisis*, pp. 191–3.

126 Colley, *In Defiance*, p. 120.

127 W. Michael, *England Under George I. The Beginnings of the Hanoverian Dynasty*, Westport, Connecticutt, repr. 1981, pp. 119–29.

128 Fritz, *English Ministers and Jacobitism*, pp. 51–4.

129 Monod, *Jacobitism*, pp. 173–92.

130 Michael, *Beginnings of the Hanoverian Dynasty*, pp. 145–6, 154.

131 Sedgwick, *House of Commons*, II, pp. 562–3.

132 Michael, *Beginnings of the Hanoverian Dynasty*, pp. 137–45.

133 Petrie, *Jacobite Movement*, pp. 132–3.

134 J. Baynes, *The Jacobite Rising of 1715*, 1970, pp. 83–125.

135 These figures are based on an estimated Scottish population of c. 1 million, of which rather less than 25 per cent would have been males between the ages of 16 and 60.

136 E. Gregg, 'The Jacobite career of John, Earl of Mar', in Cruickshanks, *Ideology and Conspiracy*, pp. 179–82.

137 Baynes, *Jacobite Rising of 1715*, pp. 64–7.

138 HMC Stuart, I, pp. 376–7, 430: the Old Pretender to Berwick, 23 July and 2 October 1715 ns; I, pp. 443–4: the Old Pretender to Bolingbroke, 21 October 1715 ns.

139 Baynes, *Jacobite Rising of 1715*, pp. 139–54. Cf. the Jacobite army's strength according to A. and H. Tayler, *1715. The Story of the Rising*, 1936, p. 95.
   140 Baynes, *Jacobite Rising of 1715*, pp. 162–82.

4

A European cause and its defeat, 1716–1759

The collapse of the rebellion in Scotland was inevitably followed by a lengthy period of mutual recrimination within the Jacobite movement. The Scots accused the English of faintheartedness, the English lambasted the Scots for setting off the rebellion before they were ready, everyone blamed the French, or the Spanish or the papacy, etc., for not having provided troops and money. The first tangible result of these internecine disputes was the Old Pretender's dismissal of Bolingbroke as Secretary of State, on the grounds that he had not been energetic enough in sending supplies and help to Scotland.[1] In his place James appointed Mar. This was undoubtedly one of the most disastrous appointments he ever made. Mar was an embittered man who had wagered his future prospects on the outcome of the revolt and lost. Moreover, he was disliked by most of his fellow-Scots and detested by the English Jacobites.[2] Nonetheless Mar recognised the seminal truth that lay at the heart of the Jacobites' defeat in 1715: in order to beat the established order in Britain they had to have the support of a major European power.

It was not simply a question of finding a supplier of money and munitions (although these were vital considerations); a major European power's support opened up a whole range of possibilities that were otherwise unavailable. Any great power that overtly supported the Jacobites was bound to be at war with Britain. In turn, this implied at least the possibility of an invasion to bolster any Jacobite rebellion. Even if the friendly power in question did not have the resources to launch such an operation, it could nonetheless tie down a large part of the British army. Hanover was highly vulnerable to conventional military operations, and Gibraltar and Minorca likewise offered a relatively easy way to distract any British government's attention. With the British army pinned down defending the Hanoverians' Continental possessions or Britain's overseas bases, the prospects of a successful Jacobite rebellion were much enhanced. As well, hostilities with a major European power with a fleet would force the Royal Navy to concentrate its forces in case of an attack – thus preventing it from thoroughly blockading the part of the British Isles in which the rebellion occurred. Slipping ships through even a weakened blockade was never easy, but it at least offered the rebels some prospect of supplies and reinforcements. Just as important as these straitly military considerations, an alliance with a major European power offered the Jacobites money and diplomatic backing of an order far removed from anything they could scrape together from their own resources.

The Jacobites also faced a gathering problem which bore directly on the need to find a great power backer, and gave the search for one steadily increasing urgency. For, in a sense, they were working against the clock. The Jacobites knew all too well that the longer the Hanoverian regime was in control, the more difficult it would become to overthrow. As George Lockhart of Carnwath lamented in 1728:

> . . .whilst no party is acting for his [the Old Pretender's] interest, no projects formed, nothing done to keep up the spirits of the people, the old race drops off by degrees and a new one sprouts up, who having no particular byass to the King, as knowing litle more of him than what the public news papers bear, enter on the stage with a perfect indifference, at least coolness, towards him and his cause, which consequently must daylie languish and in process of time be tottally forgot.[3]

Inevitably, as Hanoverian–Whig rule became 'normal', and hence developed ideological and emotional roots in the hearts, minds and pockets of Britain's population, Jacobitism was further and further marginalised.[4] This necessarily imparted more and more desperation to the Jacobites' efforts to find an external backer and stage a successful uprising 1716–54. They had to do so before the vicissitudes of time and despair eroded their base of support beyond repair.

Solving the military problem, i.e. finding a great power backer able to supply the means with which to overcome the Hanoverian regime's professional soldiery, was thus the key to the Jacobites' success or failure. Consequently, while the Jacobite court and the exile community tried to find a Continental backer for a Jacobite restoration, the Jacobites in Britain based virtually all their plans for an insurrection on the assumption that a Jacobite rising would be in support of an invasion by regular troops.[5] Jacobite politics and such strategic thinking as was carried on over the next 45 years accordingly revolved around which potential backers were showing interest in, or should be approached by the Jacobites with a view to negotiating an alliance. The Hanoverian regime was well aware of what the Jacobites were after, and correspondingly used its diplomatic machine and espionage networks to try to thwart their activities as far as possible. Thus the half-century of struggle between the rival governments following the failure of the '15 has a 'cold war' flavour to it. Each sought secretly to engage the support of ministers and favourites at virtually every European court. Jacobite and Hanoverian agents spied on, and occasionally attempted to murder, each other. Letters were intercepted, messengers and trusted confidantes suborned. The Jacobites were of course, heavily outclassed, and the British authorities consequently prevailed most of the time.[6] But on two occasions (1718–19 and 1744–6) they did not, and in both instances the eventual outcome was an attempt to invade the British Isles buttressed by a Jacobite rising in the designated landing area. For the Jacobites did have one thing of great value to offer a Continental ally already at war with Britain: a fifth column with which to paralyse or overthrow its enemy.

Rebellion as a tool of statecraft in eighteenth-century Europe

In order to understand why the great powers of Europe and the Whig regime in Britain took the Jacobite threat so seriously when the Jacobites' organisation, security and planning are prima facie so amateurish, we must briefly digress from a strict consideration of the Jacobite cause to look at the wider question of the role of rebellion in international relations in the eighteenth century; for therein lay the Jacobites' power. Given the inherently bellicose nature of eighteenth-century dynastic politics,[7] the British government rightly feared what the Jacobites were capable of precipitating abroad as much as, if not more than, anything they might do to assault the Hanoverian regime at home. Likewise those Continental great powers who considered allying with the Jacobites did not see them simply as cannon-fodder, but rather as a force which had the potential, literally, to destroy their British opponents.

These perceptions were firmly based on experience. All those involved in dealing with the Jacobites between 1715 and the 1760s were reared in the traditions of late-sixteenth- and seventeenth-century statecraft. And although statesmen always professed abhorrence of rebels and rebellion, the siren voices of religion and *realpolitick* nearly always overwhelmed their, doubtless genuine, repugnance. Thus Elizabeth I of England gave ill-tempered succour to Philip II of Spain's Dutch rebels for the second half of her reign. Philip, despite his ostensible outrage at Elizabeth's dirty tactics, showed little compunction about secretly supporting English Catholic plotters who planned to murder her and in sending what arms and monies he could spare to aid Hugh O'Neill in Ireland. His grandson, Philip IV, did nothing to prevent Gaelic Irish troops employed in the Army of Flanders from returning home in a body under their commander, Owen Roe O'Neill, to support the Irish rebels of 1641, despite the fact he and Charles I were theoretically on friendly terms. In the same vein Mazarin overcame his disgust with the regime that had executed Charles I sufficiently well to ally with it against Spain between 1656–60, and Louis XIV openly supported both the revolt of the Portuguese Braganzas against the Spanish Habsburgs and the rebellions raised by Imre Thokolly and Francis Rackozi against their Austrian cousins in Hungary.

What consistently lured the statesmen of seventeenth-century Europe into setting aside their scruples with regard to making use of domestic rebels was, more than anything else, the devastating effects on contemporary great powers of serious internecine strife. The 'Time of Troubles' in Russia traumatised the Russian political nation and put the Muscovite state out of serious contention in the great power game for nearly half a century. The once mighty Polish empire was permanently weakened by the Chmielnicki revolt of the 1650s. The decline of the Spanish Habsburg empire was directly attributable to its defeat at the hands of Dutch and Portuguese rebels and the exhausting, bitter struggle to reconquer Catalonia. Most pertinently of all, the impressive military machine James II had implicitly threatened to throw into the Continental balance of power on the side of Catholic France was brought low by a small invasion, assisted by a nationwide rebellion, in England in 1688.

The strategic attractions of using domestic rebels to destabilise enemy polities and thus achieve one's own objectives were enhanced by the chronic stalemate in conventional military operations that set in in the late seventeenth century. The military revolution of the mid-seventeenth century created formidably effective military institutions and organisations for the states of Europe.[8] So effective indeed, that no power wishing to be a major player could afford not to assume the crushing financial burdens implicit in the professional standing armies and navies created by pioneers like Gustavus Adolphus and Michel Le Tellier. The great powers of Europe correspondingly scrambled to re-equip and reorganise their armies and navies, and rebuild their fortresses, along French or Swedish lines. And by the end of the seventeenth century all the major states of Europe: France, Spain, the Netherlands, the Austrian Habsburgs, Brandenburg–Prussia, Denmark, Sweden and Britain, had successfully done so. Ironically, while this gave each of these states an overwhelming advantage when it came into conflict with a state that could not or would not modernise its forces, it acted too to offset any but the most overwhelming advantage when they confronted each other. When generals as brilliant as Marlborough and Prince Eugene faced mediocrities like Marshal Tallard a decisive outcome was still just about possible (though it is worth noting that Marlborough and Eugene were never able to pull off quite such a devastating victory as Blenheim ever again), but in the normal run of campaigning battles between the new model armies were rarely decisive and sieges were costly and frustrating. The military organisations created by the military revolution effectively tended to neutralise incompetence and thus render the armies and navies of the period much of a muchness with respect to one another.

In such circumstances it was to be expected that statesmen looking for a means to strike a decisive blow against rival powers should seek to promote internal unrest. It alone offered the prospect of knocking their enemies out of the great power game. And herein lay the Jacobites' appeal. For there was nothing like them anywhere else in Europe. Moreover, because the British government too was well aware of the implicit threat effective use of the Jacobite card posed to the established order, they were eminently blackmailable on the subject. Even if some of Britain's competitors actually regarded the Jacobites with scorn or disliked their religious complexion, the mere rumour that a given power was considering an alliance was likely to produce diplomatic overtures, efforts to reach accommodation on outstanding griev- ances, etc., on the part of the Hanoverian regime. From the point of view of the Continental powers this made the Jacobite card just too useful to be ignored. We must accordingly consider the last 45 years of active Jacobitism in a much broader, European context than the first 26.

France

The exiled Stuarts always looked to France for aid before all others. Since France was the foremost Catholic power in Europe, possessed the largest army, had a long tradition of rivalry with England and, of all the Jacobite's potential allies, was most proximate to the British Isles, this is not surprising. What is perplexing is the, at times irrational, persistence with which the Jacobites sought a French alliance. The roots of this dogged refusal to be discouraged by repeated snubs – and even betrayals[9] – lay very deep. James II and his son, and most of their inner coterie of advisers, admired Louis XIV and were bedazzled by the state he had built (see document 4). They believed the rhetoric of French absolutism, and consequently believed too that any French monarch could harness, if he wished, the entire resources of France to the Jacobite cause. The rulers of France were of course more aware of their *de facto* limitations, but tended to obscure flaws in the mighty edifice of the French state by presenting refusals to help mendicant clients like the Stuarts as arising from hidden policy rather than ministerial obstruction and institutional weakness. As a result, even after Louis XIV had formally repudiated his ties with the Old Pretender and expelled him and his court from France in 1713, Jacobite policy continued to revolve around France and French politics.

The problem confronting Jacobite emissaries and their master from 1716 onwards was a basic concordance of interests between the rulers of France and the Hanoverian regime in Britain. When Louis XIV died in 1715 he left as his heir his sickly five–year-old great-grandson. The future Louis XV was not expected to survive, and therefore the eyes of the French political nation were firmly fixed on the question of who would succeed him when he died. Louis XIV's will laid down that his nephew, the Duc d'Orléans, was to act as regent during the minority of Louis XV. Orléans was also the next heir to the throne of France in the event of Louis XV's death – provided the renunciation of his own right to succeed to the throne of France made by Philip V of Spain (Louis XIV's grandson) in 1712 was good in French law. Opinion on the subject was understandably divided. What was certain was that if Louis XV died while France was at war with Britain Orléans's claim to succeed him, based as it was on a peace treaty France had been forced to accept because of a combination of defeats and exhaustion at the hands of Britain and its allies, was likely to be challenged by Philip V. Orléans therefore had a distinct interest in maintaining the peace of Europe. By the same token, George I, only recently installed and neurotically concerned for the safety of Hanover in the event of another war, was not looking for renewed hostilities with France. Out of this confluence of interest in maintaining the status quo in international affairs, came one of the most pragmatic, and successful, diplomatic realignments of the eighteenth century: the Anglo-French alliance of 1716. Under the terms of the agreement both parties committed themselves to not aiding each other's enemies, and to maintaining the Utrecht settlement by force if necessary.[10]

The alliance, negotiated secretly by James Stanhope with Orléans's agent, the Abbé Dubois, was to endure for nearly 25 years; an era dubbed 'L'Hégémonie Anglaise' by some nationalistic French historians. The epithet is unfair. France gained a necessary breathing space, and given that both sides were committed to acting as the *gendarmes* of Europe, its intrinsic military might ensured France was always an equal partner in the arrangement.[11] The upshot of the new Anglo-French axis in European affairs for the Jacobites was much less happy. For the next generation Jacobite operations in the country closest to Britain and containing the largest, wealthiest and most powerful exile community had to be conducted in the most clandestine manner possible. Many of Orléans's ministers, and even on occasion the Regent himself, appear to have retained some sympathy for the Jacobite cause, which meant in practice they tried not to take official notice of Jacobite activity. When it was forced on their attention, or the British government demanded that Orléans act, however, they moved quickly and efficiently, which badly handicapped Jacobite operations until the alliance irretrievably broke down in the early 1740s.[12]

The deleterious effect the Anglo-French alliance had on Jacobite intrigues is best illustrated by its impact on two of them: the Atterbury plot of 1720–2 and the Cornbury plot of 1734–5. The Atterbury plot takes its name from the principal organiser of the conspiracy: Francis Atterbury, Bishop of Rochester and a passionately High Tory. The plan was that while the general election due in 1722 was being held there would be a rising in London. On the first news of the coup the English Tories, already in the country tending their constituencies, would summon their loyal tenants, servants, kinsmen and friends to arms, secure their localities, then join in a grand march on London.[13] The march on London, which as the centre of all wealth and authority in Hanoverian England was vital to the regime's survival, was to be reinforced by a landing in southern England by volunteers from the Irish regiments of the French army, led by the French-naturalised Irish general Arthur Dillon. These were to provide the crucial inner core of professionals necessary to organise the putative Jacobite army into some semblance of a fighting force.[14]

It will be obvious from the foregoing that the cooperation, or, at the very least, the willingness to turn a blind eye, of the French government was the lynchpin of the conspiracy. Moreover, for purely practical reasons it was necessary for the Jacobites to coordinate their plans through a central agency outside the British Isles. That way some semblance of security could be maintained, and money and material requirements secretly amassed well away from the spies and informers who prowled the highways and byways of English Tory society. Since there was a large exile community there – including a number of successful bankers willing to invest in a Jacobite rebellion – and many French officials were sympathetic, Paris was the obvious choice for such an over-seas base. The French government could not, however, given the Regent Orléans's own interests (to say nothing of the Anglo-French alliance), allow the conspiracy to continue once it had been obliged to take official notice of it, and it certainly could not condone French troops taking leave to go and fight as volunteers in an uprising in Britain.

The outcome was predictable from the start. As soon as Cardinal Dubois was obliged officially to take notice of the plot (after the

French government received a request for military assistance from the exiled court), he informed the British ambassador. The British government promptly began intercepting letters directed overseas and in addition despatched an agent, Colonel Charles Churchill, to Paris. There he bullied the *eminence grise* of the conspiracy, the Earl of Mar, who was hoping to work his passage home, into sending incriminating letters to the architects of the plot in England.[15] Orléans also specifically forbade the soldiers and officers of the Irish regiments from taking any further part, and moved the regiments away from the Channel coast to reduce the temptation to indulge in unsanctioned military activity. In consequence the Atterbury plot collapsed in a welter of arrests, denunciations and flights abroad.[16] In the end, however, only one of the major conspirators, the lawyer Christopher Layer, was executed, although Atterbury and Lord North and Grey were also formally ordered into exile by an act of pains and penalties.

The Cornbury plot of 1733–5 was hatched by the eponymous Lord Cornbury, heir to the Earl of Clarendon, in response to the widespread opposition to the government revealed by the Excise Crisis of 1733–4. His partners in the conspiracy were none other than the French ambassador to Britain, the Comte de Chavigny, and Cardinal Fleury's right-hand man, Secretary of State Chauvelin, in Paris.[17] Walpole had annoyed the French government by his handling of the negotiations for the second treaty of Vienna with the Habsburgs, during which he had abused their trust and neglected France's interests, and the public disorders associated with the Excise Crisis convinced Chavigny, and eventually Chauvelin, that the Hanoverian regime was on its last legs.[18] Correspondingly, Chauvelin was willing to listen to a proposal for an attack on Britain designed to place the Old Pretender on the throne. The keystone of the scheme was a French invasion of southern England, designed to draw off government troops in London and the provinces. The Jacobites in the capital and the localities would then rise and seize control of the country.[19] Chauvelin duly presented the scheme to Louis XV's inner cabinet, where the sceptical Fleury ensured it was rejected. Chavigny, whose activities had caught the attention of the British authorities, was subsequently recalled in semi-disgrace, and Chauvelin, who had incurred the jealousy of Fleury as a result of his initiative, found himself effectively demoted in terms of his status and authority within Louis XV's government.[20] Cornbury abandoned Jacobite politics and retired to his country estates to continue the process of turning himself into a paragon of good taste.

The pattern seems clear. In 1720–3 and again in 1733–5 Britain was recovering from a major political crisis. The Atterbury plotters intended to exploit the anger felt within and without the political nation towards the government, and by implication the Hanoverian dynasty, over the South Sea Bubble scandal. Likewise in 1733–4 Cornbury and his associates planned to use the popular outrage at Walpole's Excise Scheme to mobilise support for a Jacobite revolution. Both crises looked promising from the point of view of contemporary opponents of the Hanoverian regime, and dangerous from the point of view of its defenders. It is possible that a well-planned and determined revolt, supported by France with arms and men *might* have overthrown the established order in Britain. What is certain is that on each occasion the French government's interest in maintaining peaceful relations with Britain overbore the temptation to exploit the fleeting, hazardous opportunities political crises in Britain opened up. And without some kind of support from outside forces, the Jacobites were unwilling to act.

In one way the Cornbury conspiracy did indicate a change in attitudes to the Jacobites' advantage. Louis XV's inner council rejected the scheme – but it considered it first. This was symptomatic of the general trend in Anglo-French relations throughout the 1730s. By then France had recovered from its early eighteenth-century travails, and Louis XV and his ministers were beginning to suspect that Britain was getting more out of the long peace than France. In consequence there was a steady cooling of relations. When Britain went to war with Louis XV's Bourbon kinsman, Philip V of Spain, at the end of the decade, France decisively shifted its diplomatic position against Britain and in support of Spain.[21] The Jacobites, ever optimistic interpreters of such shifts and changes in French policy, started trying to work on the growing *froideur* between the two powers in the late 1730s. In 1737 John Gordon of Glenbucket tried sounding Fleury out with a proposal for an invasion backed by a Highland rising of various clans. Fleury evinced no great interest in the proposal, but this does not seem to have discouraged Lord Sempill, who from 1738 assumed the position of 'official' Jacobite agent at the French court. From 1738 to 1743, Sempill diligently lobbied Louis XV's ministers in an effort to persuade them to support a Jacobite rising.[22] When an open rupture between Britain and France finally developed in 1740-1, as both powers adopted opposite sides in the War of the Austrian Succession, Sempill was well placed to follow up the overtures he had already made.

The situation in Britain appeared propitious too. In January 1742, after repeated military failure in the war against Spain, an uneasy alliance of Patriot Whigs and Tories finally succeeded in forcing Walpole to resign. The Country opposition's victory over the 'Robinocracy' was somewhat marred, however, by the prompt desertion of William Pulteney and his Whig followers in a scramble to carve themselves a piece of the patronage pie Walpole had left behind. Angry and embittered at yet another example of Whig cupidity, many of the Tories began once again to bethink themselves of the 'King over the water'.[23]

The first tangible result of this was a message sent to Sempill by a group of leading Tories (the Duke of Beaufort, the Earl of Barrymore, Lord Orrery, Sir Watkin Williams Wynn, Sir John Hynde Cotton and Sir Robert Abdy) in the spring of 1743, asking him to approach the French government on their behalf with an invitation to invade England on behalf of the Old Pretender. Cardinal Fleury had finally died (aged 90) in January 1743 and his former *sous-ministre*, Amelot de Chaillou, responded favourably to the request for help. To establish the group's bona fides, Louis XV and his ministers agreed to send the king's Master of Horse, James Butler, a cousin of Ormond, to England to assess the situation on the pretext of buying horses for the royal stables. He duly toured southern England between August and October 1743, meeting Tory leaders, being shown lists of expected supporters, discussing the size of the proposed invasion force, and so on, before returning to Versailles to report to Louis XV personally. Louis appears to have been convinced that the Tories were genuine, for in November 1743 he finally ordered his ministers and generals to prepare an invasion of England in support of the Jacobite cause.[24]

It was planned as another winter surprise attack, scheduled for mid-February 1744. Approximately 10,000 French troops under the command of the Protestant Marshal de Saxe were to force-march from their winter quarters to invasion barges secretly accumulated on the Channel coast. There they would be joined by Charles

Edward Stuart, brought incognito into France to head the invasion force, and guided by pilots the English Jacobites were to provide, they would debark for a short crossing to Maldon in Essex. In Essex de Saxe and Charles Edward were to be joined by as many of the local Tories as could quickly reach them and immediately march on London. Given that as late as 13 February the British government was still unaware of what the naval preparations underway in France's main naval bases portended, the main thrust of the plan must be regarded as having come very close to success (whether or not the Hanoverians would have lost the ensuing civil war is another matter entirely). Though many putative Jacobites were promptly arrested when the Pelham ministry discovered what was afoot, it only went irrecoverably awry on 24 February when a terrible storm, one of the worst of the century, blew apart Admiral Norris's and Admiral Roquefeuil's fleets, which were just about to do battle for control of the Channel. Of Norris's fleet of 19 ships one was sunk and 5 put out of action. Roquefeuil ran before the storm back to Brest. More importantly, virtually all the supplies and equipment de Saxe had painstakingly accumulated over the previous six months were destroyed. On 28 February Charles Edward was officially informed that the invasion had been cancelled.[25]

For the next year and a half Charles Edward languished impotently in France. The pleasures of bed, bottle and board at the expense of the French government doubtless compensated to some extent, but he always wanted to cut a figure as a man of action and there was no possibility of him doing so for the foreseeable future. With the abandonment of the projected invasion of England, those of Louis XV's ministers who had favoured such a descent upon the enemy were eclipsed by other advisers, most notably the Duc de Noailles, who had opposed such a distraction all along. They favoured instead a conventional military attack on the Austrian Netherlands, and it was to this that de Saxe and his army were committed in the summer of 1744. Charles Edward was meanwhile shuffled from minister to minister, interview to interview with the dignitaries and flunkies of the French court. Basically, Louis XV and his ministers could not make up their minds what to do with him. The English invasion for which he had been summoned was indefinitely postponed. The Noailles faction did not want to offend France's German Protestant allies by too obviously favouring the

Catholic Stuarts, so he could not be allowed openly to campaign alongside de Saxe or any other French general. As well, Charles Edward's prickly sense of honour and his constant badgering of French ministers for a definite commitment to another invasion soon began to irritate them. As relations deteriorated between the two Charles Edward correspondingly began researching some form of initiative independent of the French.[26]

The upshot was a cleverly constructed piece of adventurism. Early in 1744, piqued at the French exclusion of Scotland from any part in the invasion scheme, a small number of clan chieftains had intimated to Charles Edward in a message sent via John Murray of Broughton that they would rise to greet him even if he arrived with only 3,000 French troops. With the help of a small coterie of Jacobite exiles, Charles Edward now proceeded to take them up on their offer. While continuing to harass the French government with demands for a renewal of the invasion preparations and money to sustain his expensive social life, Charles and a consortium of Nantes privateers headed by Antoine Walsh (the biggest shipowner in Nantes) concocted a plan whereby Charles Edward would make a dash for Scotland with only two ships. Funded by the exiled bankers John Waters and Aeneas Macdonald, the final plan had him arriving in the western highlands of Scotland at the head of 700 volunteers from the Irish Régiment de Clare, plus 20 small cannon, 11,000 stand of arms, 2,000 broadswords and a substantial quantity of gunpowder. On paper this was a promising inner core for a Highland revolt. In actuality it was an incredible gamble. Charles Edward was well aware that if the French authorities or his father caught wind of what was being planned they would stop him. He therefore kept all knowledge of his involvement in Walsh's preparations for what was apparently a normal privateering cruise, well hidden. The first news the French government had of what was going on was a personal letter from Charles Edward to Louis XV announcing his departure and asking him for help in sustaining the rebellion.[27]

The sad story of the '45 is one that revolves around the failure of the French government to organise an invasion of England while the rebels were advancing, or sustain them with substantial reinforcements when they were forced to retreat back to Scotland. The need for prompt aid became, moreover, critical as a result of an unfortunate encounter during Charles Edward's voyage to

Scotland. His small force was packed aboard the small ship-of-the-line *Elisabeth* and the frigate *Du Teillay*. On the fourth day of the voyage they encountered HMS *Lion*, a vessel nearly as large and well armed as the *Elisabeth*, which the *Lion* duly proceeded to fight. The action was a draw, but both ships were badly damaged and the *Elisabeth* was forced to turn back, taking with her Charles Edward's 700–strong force of professional soldiery and virtually all his carefully accumulated munitions. Nothing could have more clearly revealed how risky a venture he was embarked on than the results of this single encounter. Nonetheless he insisted on continuing his voyage, and, after being briefly chased by another Royal Navy frigate in the Irish Sea, made landfall on the Isle of Eriskay on 23 July.[28]

Almost as soon as he landed Charles Edward was firmly rebuffed by almost all the 'Associators' who had invited him to invade Scotland in 1743. Without French troops and a good supply of arms and ammunition, the clan chieftains claimed, there was no prospect of victory, so he might as well go home. Nothing daunted, Charles Edward embarked on a lightning campaign of personal diplomacy, and one-by-one persuaded most of the long-established Jacobites among them to relent and raise their clans for him. It is a measure of how apprehensive the chieftains were though, that two of the most important additions to Charles Edward's army, Donald Cameron of Lochiel and Cluny Macpherson, had virtually to be bought by Charles Edward. Both men insisted on, and received, pledges of compensation before they turned out.[29] By the end of the month too, the administration in Edinburgh had received such overwhelming evidence of a rebellion mustering in the Highlands that it overcame their initial incredulity, and Sir John Cope and a small field army were despatched to put down the rising. Cope was a very ordinary general and Charles Edward easily outmanoeuvred him in the eastern Highlands, recruiting busily all the while, before breaking out into the lowlands and seizing Perth.[30]

By this stage of the campaign the Jacobites were doing very well indeed. They were between Cope and his bases, and the whole of lowland Scotland lay before them, well-nigh undefended. Charles Edward therefore briskly advanced on Edinburgh, which the Jacobites took (except for the castle) by subterfuge on 17 September. Cope by this time had taken ship from Inverness and transported his army south of Edinburgh to disembark at Dunbar.

Determined to retrieve his reputation, Cope then advanced back north towards Edinburgh, meeting the exuberant Jacobite army on its southward march at Prestonpans on 20 September. There the Jacobite army swiftly disposed of its opponent. In a few minutes Cope's force of about 2,500 men was utterly destroyed by Charles Edward's of roughly the same size.[31] It was the decisive lift Charles Edward needed to get the rebellion well off the ground. To Charles Edward's credit, even after such a spectacular victory he recognised that without French intervention the rebels could not win, and one of his first acts after the battle was to send another messenger to France bearing the good tidings and pleading for a prompt invasion of England.[32]

Charles had been sending such messages almost since the moment of his arrival in Scotland.[33] He appears to have been convinced, and in turn to have convinced the clan chieftains who turned their men out to fight for him, that his raising an insurrection in Scotland would break the vicious, frustrating cycle whereby the French demanded a rebellion before they invaded and the Jacobites demanded an invasion before they rebelled.[34] Charles's logic was irrefutable – he had done what the French government had always demanded – but his strategic vision was poor. Having committed themselves to a major land offensive in Flanders (which was yielding splendid results thanks to de Saxe), the French government, even if it immediately and wholeheartedly committed itself to an invasion of England, could not deliver such an invasion in less than two to three months. But the Jacobites in Scotland needed such an offensive a lot sooner if they were not to be overwhelmed by the sheer weight of men and material the Hanoverian regime would shortly be able to bring to bear. If the French had begun preparations for an invasion when Charles Edward sailed they might have been ready before the odds against the Jacobites began to mount beyond the point of no return. Instead of doing so, however, Louis XV and his ministers prudently held their fire until the rebellion proved viable – in late September, after Prestonpans. Delays in deciding where to invade and how many troops to commit held up preparations for a further month, so that it was November before preparations began in earnest.[35]

Meanwhile Charles and his council, having quickly collected further reinforcements, were deadlocked for nearly a month on the question of whether or not to invade England. Charles Edward passionately advocated this strategy on the grounds that the English Jacobites could then safely rise and join him, automatically triggering the French invasion they all agreed was vital. Opposed to him were a party led by Lord George Murray, the military genius of the '45, who favoured a more cautious, defensive strategy, whereby the Jacobites would concentrate on consolidating their hold on Scotland until the French invaded. By a margin of one vote, probably secured by Charles's express declaration that he had English Tory assurances of a rising if he appeared in England in arms (which he did not), he persuaded the Jacobite leadership to agree to an invasion.[36] The Jacobite army, now grown to at least 4,500, duly crossed the frontier close by Carlisle on 8 November.

The swift march into the heart of England that followed has been described as a second Anabasis, after the fighting retreat home of Xenophon's 10,000 Greek mercenaries from the heart of the Persian empire in 401 BC.[37] This is to overstate both its significance and the odds against the Jacobite army. Nevertheless the march from Carlisle to Derby and the retreat therefrom were deftly handled and undoubtedly redound to the credit of Lord George Murray. Indeed, it is highly ironic that the man most vehemently opposed to the whole expedition was the man who saved the army from envelopment and almost certain annihilation on several occasions. Unfortunately for the Jacobites, Charles was aware of his debt to Murray too, and bitterly resented it. He could not brook sustained opposition to his will, still less reasoned, cogent criticism of his plans, and thus by the time the crucial council of war came, at Derby on 5 December, it was well known that Charles and his best general were barely on speaking terms.[38]

By the time of the council, Lord George Murray had succeeded in outmanoeuvring both Hanoverian armies, under the command of Field-Marshal George Wade and the Duke of Cumberland respectively, so that the Jacobite army was poised to strike at London. All that lay between it and the capital was a mob of very nervous militia at Finchley.[39] Elsewhere events seemed to be working out equally propitiously. In France the Marquis d'Argenson, who was in charge of administering preparations for the invasion, and the Duc de Richelieu, who was to command it, were rushing through the final stages of an *ad hoc* amphibious operation so as to be ready to invade by mid-December.[40] Meanwhile the

English Jacobite leadership, who had stubbornly remained quiescent all through the march southwards on the grounds that they wanted a French invasion before they would turn out, had finally worked their courage up to the sticking point. A messenger from Lord Barrymore and Sir Watkin Williams Wynn, pledging their support if Charles Edward reached London, was on his way to Derby at the time of the fateful council.[41] Had the chieftains but known it, the Jacobite army was poised to achieve at least a short-term victory.

At the council of war Charles's lies about his assurances of an English uprising and French invasion were finally exposed (see document 5). He was forced to admit he had had no contact with the English Jacobites since before he landed at Moidart, thereby revealing that the whole expedition into England was based on nothing more than Charles Edward's supposition of what the French and English would do if the Scottish Jacobites marched southward.[42] That his gamble may have been about to pay off is only apparent to historians operating with the benefit of hindsight. To the clan chieftains on the spot in Derby it looked as if Charles's mendacity had left them out on the end of a very slim limb. Their concern was crystallised by a false report of a third, entirely fictitious, Hanoverian army closing in on them on top of the two they had already bypassed. The final vote on whether to retreat or not went overwhelmingly against Charles Edward: he was the only person on the council of war to vote in favour of continuing to advance. He promptly threw a tantrum and vowed never to consult such a council again.[43]

Nonetheless the army retreated. Charles effectively refused to take any further part in running the campaign: he threw a monumental pet, ostentatiously snubbed and obstructed his commanders and consoled himself with strong liquor.[44] Fortunately for the Jacobite army it still had Lord George Murray, who by dint of some quite brilliant feints and even more careful planning managed to extricate it virtually intact.[45] Meanwhile the English Jacobites went to ground once again and the French continued their preparations to invade. Despite gathering pessimism on the part of Richelieu, confronted by the inevitable breakdowns in logistics and planning created by throwing together a complex operation like a cross-Channel invasion in a hurry, there was a real prospect of a successful French landing between 20 and 24 December. The winds that would have blown Richelieu's expedition across to England obligingly pinned Admiral Vernon, who had been busily disrupting Richelieu's preparations by attacking his convoys of transport ships, against the Kentish coast. All seemed set for the long-awaited French invasion: 10,000 troops led by Richelieu and Charles's brother Henry Benedict were primed to land. Yet nothing happened. News of the Jacobite army's retreat from Derby increased Richelieu's misgivings, he found Prince Henry's ostentatious piety offensive, his commanders fell to bickering among themselves, Vernon resumed station off Boulogne and stepped up his raiding, and to round it all off the weather turned against him. By 2 January not even a direct order from Louis XV to invade immediately could move Richelieu, so far was he sunk in despair and defeatism. By 1 February all hope of an invasion of England had passed and the army assembled at Boulogne was broken up.[46]

The '45 in Britain, however, was not yet over. Though they had withdrawn from England, the Jacobites still held Scotland, and over the next two months, reinforced by a trickle of men and munitions from France that evaded the Royal Navy's blockade, the Jacobite army was able to hold its own. This, and especially the Jacobite victory at the battle of Falkirk in January, was largely due to the efforts of Lord George Murray, since Charles Edward was still sulking in his tent.[47] The petulant prince only finally emerged at the end of January to protest the army's retreat northwards in the face of the steadily mounting odds it was facing in southern Scotland.[48] Overruled this time too, he retreated once more into drunken sulkiness. The final denouement came in April, when, despite the protests of his officers, Charles insisted on fighting an orthodox defensive action at Culloden. The Jacobite army was decisively defeated and Charles Edward promptly abandoned it.[49] It is a testament to the army's discipline and potential as a fighting force that even after the defeat the stragglers and unengaged units rallied at the agreed rendezvous in the event of such an emergency, and only dispersed when ordered to do so by Charles. Likewise it is a testimony to the prince's character that he departed blaming everything on the treachery of his officers.[50]

The '45 was over, but France's involvement with the Jacobite cause was not yet done. While the Duke of Cumberland's forces ruthlessly harried the miserable clansmen for having followed their superiors into rebellion, Louis XV ordered every effort be made to rescue the fugitive prince and as many of the chieftains as possible. After some appropriately romantic escapes, including a period accompanying the legendary Flora Macdonald as a lady's maid named 'Betty Burke', Charles was picked up and transported back to France and safety in September 1746. There he was given a hero's welcome. The prince was duly flattered, but seems not to have lost sight of the main event, and was soon badgering the French government to provide him with troops and ships to mount a renewed assault on the Hanoverian regime. Louis XV and his ministers were initially inclined to listen – from their point of view Charles had achieved miracles with virtually nothing, so what might he achieve if they backed him up from the start? – but France's commitment to the war in Flanders eventually precluded operations elsewhere in 1747. By then too, France was increasingly war-weary, and the economy was showing distinct signs of strain. To cap it all, Louis and his ministers soon began to be irritated by Charles Edward's histrionics. As a consequence, when de Saxe won a couple of stunning victories that summer, knocking the Netherlands out of the war and thereby persuading the British to offer reasonable peace terms, it was virtually inevitable that these terms would be (unenthusiastically) accepted by the French government.[51]

And of course one of Britain's pre-conditions for peace negotiations was the expulsion of Charles Edward from France. Having duly explained the regrettable necessity that he return to Italy, or otherwise leave France, the French court expected a reasonably prompt compliance. Charles simply ignored the order, and instead continued to demand military support and money to accommodate his extravagant lifestyle. Louis's ministers, perplexed at their failure to communicate the need for the prince to leave, emphatically reiterated their previous explanations and orders. Charles Edward continued blithely to ignore them. Worse, he began openly flaunting his presence in and around Paris by visiting the Opéra, attending balls, and so on, while the peace negotiations were getting underway. The British plenipotentiaries naturally complained that the French were not keeping up their side of the bargain, and Louis XV and his ministers accordingly became increasingly irate at the Jacobite prince's behaviour. Eventually the French government lost all patience with Charles Edward, and in December 1748 he was literally set upon by some burly NCOs of the royal guards while on his way to the Opéra, bundled into a carriage and incarcerated at Vincennes before being expelled from France.[52]

Relations between France and the vital element in the Jacobite cause, centred on Charles Edward (as opposed to the sedentary one centred on his father), entered their terminal stage at this point. Charles's pride was so outraged he could not bring himself even to speak to French emissaries for some time. Neither did the French government want anything to do with him. For nearly ten years the only communications between the two were conducted via the Old Pretender and his ageing shadow court in Rome, with whom the French government throughout stayed on reasonably good terms. Louis XV and his ministers continued to help individual Jacobites, and privately to support the Old Pretender and Henry Benedict, who had fled his brother's bullying to take holy orders in 1747 and was soon well on his way to being a cardinal. Otherwise they ignored Charles Edward, who by the 1750s was the only recourse for those still actively interested in the Jacobite cause.[53] In the late 1750s, confronted with defeats in Germany and the imminent loss of most of their overseas empire, the French government was again drawn into considering a Jacobite attempt, but when he met Charles the French Foreign Minister, Choiseul, was so disgusted by the prince's sodden paranoia that he abandoned the scheme.[54] Apart from a brief interlude in the early 1770s when the French government quietly supported Charles's negotiations for his marriage with Louise of Stolberg, this was the end of France's involvement with the Jacobite cause.[55] It also clearly signalled the terminal decline of the movement.

Sweden

Sweden's involvement with the Jacobites stemmed from its precarious position in the 1710s. By 1716 Sweden was entering the seventeenth year of its desperate struggle with the coalition of enemies who had first attacked it in 1700. At various times between the onset of the war and 1716 this coalition's fluctuating membership included Russia (the only constant opponent), Poland–Saxony, Denmark, Prussia, and most significantly for the purposes of this analysis, Hanover. In 1712 Hanoverian troops occupied the town of Verden, ostensibly to save it from the Danes, and in 1715 its neighbour Bremen, as the price of George I's accession to the Northern alliance against Sweden.[56] Both towns were profitable outposts of the Swedish empire, whose finances had always depended on its control of, and therefore ability to tax, the riparine traffic that passed up and down the major rivers whose outlets the Swedes controlled. The wedge of territory composing Bremen and Verden controlled the traffic on the rivers Weser and Elbe, and by 1712, as a consequence of the loss of most of its empire in the eastern Baltic, Sweden was more dependent than ever on the revenues provided by its western possessions. Persuading the Hanoverians to withdraw their forces (or otherwise compensate Sweden) correspondingly became a major objective of Swedish foreign policy.[57]

Sweden's problems were further compounded, and Swedish anger at Hanover's jackal-like behaviour considerably increased, by the Hanoverians' use of British forces on the side of the anti-Swedish coalition. From 1715, in direct contravention of the act of succession that brought his dynasty to the British throne, George I began giving the commanders of Royal Navy squadrons sent to the Baltic to convoy British merchantmen safely through the war-zone verbal instructions to do whatever they could to help the anti-Swedish coalition.[58] The Swedish navy was correspondingly hamstrung in its efforts to beat off coalition attacks on its shipping and raids on Sweden's coastline. Meanwhile, whenever Sweden's diplomats raised the question of Bremen and Verden, Hanover's emissaries would blandly offer to buy the territories at a knockdown price. In the resulting climate of hostility towards the Hanoverians it is hardly surprising to find that a number of Swedish diplomats began to consider playing the Jacobite card.[59]

The Jacobites were well aware of Sweden's difficulties and its gathering hostility towards Hanover, and had been looking for an opening to move to direct negotiations since before the '15.[60] Consequently the overtures of the Swedish ambassador to Paris, Count Sparre, drew a prompt, positive response. Within a short time the Swedish ambassador to Britain, Count Gyllenborg, and his superior, Charles XII's *eminence grise*, Baron Goertz, were deeply involved in talks with prominent Jacobites, such as Atterbury and Oxford, in Britain and France. The ostensible occasion for the exchanges that took place in 1716–17 was the negotiation of a substantial loan to be raised from among the Jacobites and their

Tory sympathisers in Britain. On the surface it was a straight-forward, if covert, commercial transaction. In actuality there was a predictable subtext: the Swedes were to provide an army of about 10,000 men to invade northern England.[61] The Swedish diplomats, while sympathetic to the Jacobites' objectives, refused definitively to commit their master to waging war on Britain, but the negotiations nonetheless proceeded.[62] The Jacobites, for their part, calculated that the gratitude of a warlord like Charles XII was a thing worth having in and of itself, and might still in the end be transformed into material aid. It is also worth noting that the prospect, however remote, of a *Protestant* king supported by a *Protestant* army restoring the Stuarts attracted both Jacobites and Tories so strongly that it almost certainly accelerated their commitment to striking a bargain with the Swedes. What better way to refute the Whigs' perennial charge that to restore the Stuarts would be to restore popery? The Old Pretender endorsed the raising of the loan, and a large sum, possibly as much as £60,000 in the end, was surreptitiously collected.[63]

In January 1717, having caught wind of what was afoot through their spies, as well as letters of Gyllenborg's intercepted on their way to Sweden, George I and his ministers ordered Gyllenborg's arrest and that his house be searched. This breach of diplomatic immunity shocked many contemporaries, but the ministry thereby secured documents sufficiently incriminating to suggest that Gyllenborg had been involved in activities that no government could tolerate.[64] He was subsequently expelled from Britain, but since the Swedes had made no formal commitment to invade on behalf of the Jacobites, only led them to believe that securing the loan would facilitate a favourable decision, open hostilities did not follow. Baron Goertz certainly knew what the Jacobites were after, and was willing to consider helping them. Charles XII almost certainly knew what was going on, but the fact that all Gyllenborg's official correspondence on the subject had been with Goertz and Sparre gave him, to use a cynical twentieth-century term: 'plausible deniability', which he made good use of.[65]

There was insufficient evidence of treason to allow the British government to proceed against the handful of Jacobite agents, such as Charles Caesar, the former Tory MP for Hertford, swept up in the arrests of those associated with the plot. Consequently negotiations with the Swedes resumed in the summer of 1717.

Nothing material transpired from these contacts, however, before Charles XII's death at the siege of the fortress of Frederiksten in the autumn of 1718.[66] Sweden effectively lost heart after the death of Charles XII, and his successor, Queen Ulrika Eleonora, made a separate peace in 1719 which ceded Bremen and Verden to Hanover, thus removing the bone of contention between Sweden and Britain. Relations between Sweden and the Jacobites nonetheless remained cordial. Gyllenborg emerged as something of a martyr-hero in post-Caroline politics, and the Swedish government even allowed the French to raise a regiment for (unacknowledged) service in Scotland during the '45.[67]

The last encounter between the two governments, in 1784, was motivated, however, not by any desire to restore Charles Edward (by then Charles 'III') to his putative thrones, but by Gustav III's obsession with the notion of gaining control of Europe's network of Freemasons. Swedish Masonic mythology ascribed to Charles Edward the secret headship of the 'Templar' Masonic order. Gustav hence believed Charles could supply him with the authority to command the allegiance of these lodges from one end of the Continent to the other. Charles Edward, who knew of the legend and that it was bogus, but was running short of drinking money, duly milked him of some ready cash and required Gustav to arrange a financial separation with his estranged 'queen', Louise of Stolberg. In a fittingly sordid end to the thoroughly exploitative relationship between Sweden and the Jacobites, Gustav successfully accomplished this, then persuaded Charles to transfer his 'authority' and promptly decamped, leaving Charles Edward waiting in vain for the lucrative payments he had been led to expect.[68]

Spain

Spain's involvement with the Jacobites after 1715 was brought on by serious policy clashes with the British government. Whereas Britain had arguably emerged as one of several victors of the War of the Spanish Succession, there could be no doubt that Spain had been comprehensively defeated. In order to obtain peace Spain had been forced to accede to the loss of virtually all its territories in Italy, the entire Spanish Netherlands, Port Mahon in Minorca and Gibraltar in Andalusia. Consequently, Spain was the most discontented of all the European states with the balance of power established by the Utrecht settlement of 1713, and sought most systematically to undermine it.[69]

For a whole raft of dynastic, religious and economic reasons France would normally have been the power Spain turned to for an alliance dedicated to overthrowing the existing international order, but, as already noted, the period 1715–31 was unusual in being one of sustained tension between the two powers. Therefore Spain had to look elsewhere. The Habsburgs were the principal beneficiaries of the Peace of Utrecht, and anyway still harboured hopes of securing the entire Spanish Habsburg inheritance, which ruled them out. The Dutch Republic was rapidly sinking to the level of a second-rank power and had too great a stake in the Utrecht settlement to want to overturn it. Britain had been the financial lynchpin of the Grand Alliance and was now reaping the rewards of its success, which put it out of consideration. Sweden, Prussia and Russia were too preoccupied with Baltic affairs to be serious contenders for an alliance. Spain was thus left facing a relatively solid inclination to maintain the status quo among the great powers of Europe. The only way to get around this obstacle would be to bring about a change of regime in one of the great powers that would favour Spanish interests and a Spanish alliance. Of all the available factions, rebels and intriguers Spain might have exploited to bring this about, the Jacobites were undoubtedly the most formidable, and in the event of success, offered the best return on Spain's investment.

Despite the seemingly tantalising advantages of a Spanish–Jacobite alliance, Cardinal Alberoni, premier minister to Philip V and Queen Elizabeth Farnese, moved very cautiously at first. His aim seems to have been to separate the Habsburgs from Britain, crush them militarily, and thus retrieve Spain's lost Italian possessions.[70] This could be achieved just as well with the cooperation of the Hanoverians as the Stuarts, and the Spanish government therefore hedged its bets. On the one hand, Alberoni wooed the new regime in Britain by proffering commercial concessions. On the other, the Spanish ambassador in Paris secretly negotiated the payment of a substantial sum (eventually amounting to the equivalent of £43,500) into the coffers of the exiled dynasty.[71] For conspirators as starved of funds as the Jacobites such generosity was bound to incur gratitude, and even after Spain and Britain signed a new commercial treaty in December 1715, the Stuart court continued to hope for Spanish succour. Philip V shrewdly encouraged it with a small, secret pension to the Old Pretender from 1716 onwards.[72]

As a result, when Spain and Britain fell out in 1717 over Spain's invasion and conquest of Sicily (awarded to the Duke of Savoy under the Utrecht settlement), Alberoni had his Jacobite card ready to hand. His use of it was precipitated by the decisive Anglo-Dutch naval victory at Cape Passaro in 1718. Ordered to prevent the Spanish fleet carrying their victorious troops onward from Sicily to the Italian mainland, Admiral Byng proceeded to destroy the Spanish armament as a fighting force.[73] A major Spanish army was thus left stranded in Sicily while French troops, mobilised under the Anglo-French alliance, massed on Spain's northern frontier preparatory to an invasion of Catalonia. In such circumstances Alberoni had to do something dramatic to redress a balance of power seemingly inexorably turning against Spain. With the ardent support of his royal master and mistress, he accordingly sent for the Old Pretender, appointed Ormond a general in the Spanish service, summoned Earl Marischal and other Scottish Jacobite exiles and set in train preparations for an invasion of the British Isles.[74]

On this occasion the perennial problem of coordinating external invasion and internal uprising was to be forthrightly bypassed. The Spanish plan envisioned a straightforward military invasion of the West Country (Ormond's former political heartland), plus a secondary uprising in the Highlands of Scotland, to be precipitated by the landing of a small Spanish force accompanied by a cadre of exiled clan chieftains.[75] It was a simple, direct plan, initially caught Britain's governors by surprise and might have caused serious problems for the fledgeling Hanoverian regime had it materialised. Fortunately for it, most of the invasion force never got any further than Cape Finisterre. Throwing together sufficient forces for the operation took longer than expected, and Ormond began to feel serious misgivings about the whole idea.[76] The fleet was only finally ready to set sail in late February 1719, which, as any contemporary seaman could have told its commanders, was the worst season of the year for storms in the Bay of Biscay region from which it was to set out. The armada duly encountered a severe storm and almost all of it was scattered and blown back onto the coast of Spain. From there it limped back into harbour, and the main expedition was shelved.[77] The secondary invasion, destined for Scotland, got through, however, giving rise to the little-known Jacobite rising of 1719.

The rebellion was handicapped from the start by dissension between Marischal, the senior Spanish officer-in-command, and the clan leaders returning from exile. The Marquess of Tullibardine (the Duke of Atholl's attainted heir) trumped Marischal with an old commission of his own issued by the Old Pretender, and then hesitated about striking quickly at the scattered Hanoverian garrisons. Instead, the force of about 1,500 clansmen and 250 Spanish regulars the rebels were able to put together dawdled in the Highlands hoping to hear news of Ormond's landing in the West Country. This gave Major-General Wightman time to assemble a rather smaller force of regulars, march down the Great Glen and corner the Jacobites at Glenshiel. The outcome of the battle was never in doubt, as Wightman intelligently used his artillery to blast the Jacobites out of their entrenchments before his infantry even came within range of the clansmen's dreaded 'Highland charge'. The clansmen and their leaders then made good their getaway, leaving the Spanish infantry to take the only option available to them: surrender.[78] Spain's military situation proceeded to deteriorate through the summer and autumn of 1719, and it was soon clear Philip V was going to have to sue for peace. Alberoni was accordingly dismissed, Ormond and the Old Pretender ordered to depart and Philip V was graciously accorded lenient terms by the victorious Quadruple Alliance (Britain, France, the Dutch Republic and the Habsburgs).[79]

Thereafter Spain's interest in the Jacobite cause took on a more desultory aspect. When the Old Pretender and his spouse, Clementina Sobieska, fell out over the appointment of a tutor for the young Jacobite princes in 1725, and subsequently over James's choice of John Hay of Cromlix, Jacobite Earl of Inverness, as his Secretary of State, the Spanish court suddenly took a great deal of interest in the proceedings. Seeing the opportunity to pose as the guardian of true, intransigent Catholicism, the Spanish court and its unofficial agent at Rome, Alberoni (who was also in Walpole's pay), seized it with both hands and openly declared in favour of the 'persecuted' Queen Clementina. Their intervention and support for Clementina's religious bigotry considerably compounded the Old Pretender's marital problems. Clementina's obduracy was reinforced by the Spanish intervention, and James's attempts at a compromise and reconciliation short of the dismissal of the offending minister were brusquely rejected. Only by parading his spotless commitment to the Catholic church (something it was always best for Jacobite princes to underplay for British consumption), was James able to persuade Pope Benedict XIII to intervene on his behalf, thereby forcing Clementina to emerge from the convent where she had taken refuge.[80] And in 1745, when from a Continental perspective it seemed as if Charles Edward might be on the brink of achieving a second restoration, the ageing Ormond revived his Spanish captain-generalship to travel to Madrid and die there pleading the Jacobite prince's cause. Whatever help the Spanish government might have been inclined to give was soon negated by the collapse of the '45 in Scotland, but Charles Edward nonetheless travelled there in hope early in 1747. He was courteously received, but as courteously refused all assistance, and left in a huff.[81] All significant contact thereupon ceased.

Russia

Russian interest in the Jacobite cause, like Spanish, stemmed from a combination of diplomatic isolation and pique. Peter the Great's new model Russian state was clearly set to emerge triumphant from the Great Northern War by 1716. There was, however, a price attached to having been the principal agent and beneficiary of the dismemberment of the Swedish empire, and Russia had already begun to pay for its victory by becoming a diplomatic pariah. Russia's success against the hitherto invincible Swedes had created by 1716 an atmosphere of apprehension in the chanceries of its neighbours. And following the Silent Sejm of 1717 in which Russian intervention reduced the kingdom of Poland effectively to vassalage, the frontier of Russian power seemed poised to extend as far as the eastern borders of Germany. The consequent nervousness of the German princes was expressed in two divergent ways, exemplified by the reactions of Prussia and Hanover to the problem. In Prussia a determined attempt was made to cultivate a good relationship with the bear to the east.[82] In Hanover, by contrast, the Electoral chancery (backed of course by Britain) tried to build up a network of alliances and understandings that would contain the Russians.[83] As a consequence, by 1716 the tsar was increasingly finding his efforts to capitalise on Russia's victory opposed by a united front of Russia's erstwhile allies in the Great Northern War.

Never a man to brook opposition, Peter I responded with a ferocious determination to exact his due reward – even contemplating abandoning his allies in favour of a new league with their original foe, Sweden. And since Hanover was the mainspring of the opposition to Russia's achieving territorial gains commensurate with its role in the allied victory, Peter and his advisers began listening as well to the urgings of the numerous exiled Scots and other Jacobite officers in Russian service. The first fruits of the tsar's new interest in the potential usefulness of the Jacobites came in the form of an offer of a marriage alliance between a Russian grandduchess (Peter's daughter Anne) and the Old Pretender, who was at that time looking for a wife. The Jacobite court politely declined the match, but energetically pursued the opening by sending Ormond to Russia to ask Peter for help. Ormond's embassy of 1717, during which he had a personal interview with the tsar, ultimately proved fruitless because Peter was unwilling to come to James's aid without a matching alliance with Spain and Sweden, but it alerted the tsar and his ministers to the potential of the Jacobite card.[84] Correspondingly, as Russo-Hanoverian relations steadily worsened then finally broke down 1718–20, Russian interest in the Jacobite cause revived.

What Peter was principally after was a Franco-Russian alliance that would leave Hanover vulnerable to a Russian offensive on land and therefore more amenable to Russian demands. As a result, the wary negotiations that resumed between the Russian ambassador to Paris, Prince Dolgoruky, and General Dillon in 1722 were based on a false premise. Peter appears to have believed that Jacobite influence in France could provide a backstairs means of sundering the Anglo-French alliance in favour of a Russo-French pact. The Jacobite court was obviously not inclined to disabuse him of this false impression, and duly sent an envoy, Colonel Daniel O'Brien (an Irish officer in French service), to Russia to press their case for an invasion of the British Isles in 1723. O'Brien pursued his mission tenaciously, secured a personal interview with the tsar, and eventually persuaded him to open direct (albeit secret) negotiations with the Old Pretender. Peter was nonetheless still absolutely determined that he would not undertake anything in favour of the Jacobites without a rapprochement with France.

Hopes on both sides were raised when Orléans died in 1724, as his successor as regent, the Duc de Bourbon, had openly sympathised with the Jacobite cause on a number of occasions. Bourbon's inclinations were outweighed by France's national interests, however, and his response to Peter's overtures was to attempt to reconcile him with George I. Bourbon failed to achieve a reconciliation, and Peter continued to cultivate his Jacobite connection until his death in 1725, but it seems unlikely that anything would have come of the negotiations.[85]

Peter's successors were obliged to retrench Russia's far-flung diplomatic and territorial ambitions while the empire recovered from its prodigious efforts under the warrior-tsar, and hence completely lost interest in the Jacobite cause. Russia occasionally featured in Jacobite plotting, but there were henceforth no contacts of any real significance.[86]

Prussia

The rise of Prussia in the late seventeenth and early eighteenth centuries was based on a few simple, achievable foreign policy objectives. These revolved around making discrete acquisitions on its existing frontiers and, more generally, presenting the Hohenzollern dynasty as staunch guardians of the Protestant cause in central Europe. The upshot of this was that until the accession of the arch-Machiavellian Frederick the Great,[87] Prussia showed not the slightest interest in helping the Jacobites. A Catholic dynasty in Britain was bound to upset the religious balance of power in Europe, and insofar as that ever threatened to become reality, Prussia was actively hostile to the Jacobite cause. Even in the late 1720s when Hanover and Prussia came into conflict over their rivalry within the Holy Roman Empire in general and north Germany in particular, Prussia did not even look into the possibility of using the Jacobite card. Some things were obviously more important than gaining an edge over a rival north German power.

Nor did this attitude immediately change with the accession of Frederick I in 1740. Frederick was to become one of the most cynical practitioners of *realpolitick* the world has ever seen, but he had nothing to gain in the 1740s by compromising Prussia's reputation as a champion of central European Protestantism.[88] The Prussian king accordingly reacted very coolly to France's support for the Jacobites 1743–6, even offering George II Prussian troops to

113

suppress the uprising at one point. Charles Edward's achievements in Scotland, however, seem to have changed Frederick's opinion of him and his cause. Notwithstanding the eventual defeat of the uprising, the Prussian monarch publicly praised Charles's generalship and wrote to him personally asking for his portrait.[89] And although Prussia's official foreign policy does not seem to have changed much, Frederick does appear to have begun favouring various exiled Jacobite officers who were employed in the Prussian service. The most important of these were the Keith brothers: the Earl Marischal himself and his brother James Keith. This apparent thawing of Prussian hostility to the exiled Stuarts was, however, more apparent than real. Although both of the Keiths played major parts in Jacobite military and diplomatic endeavours up to the 1720s, both were profoundly disillusioned with the cause by the 1740s, and consequently were more interested in making new careers for themselves overseas than in fighting their way back to Britain.[90] They were first and foremost Frederick's loyal servants, and hence the hopes their rise to power in Prussia inspired among Jacobite ministers and plotters were singularly misplaced.

The interest Frederick was evincing in the Jacobite cause was, nonetheless, too good an opportunity to miss, especially as Charles Edward was at this time determined never to work with the French government again. The Jacobite prince had spent the period 1749–51 laying the groundwork for a rising in England. To this end he had collected a small arsenal of military equipment and in 1750 personally visited London. While there, Charles conferred at length with the English Jacobite leadership, then assessed the feasibility of an assault on the Tower of London and formally converted to Anglicanism. The upshot of his conferences with the Duke of Beaufort, Lord Westmoreland and Dr William King was not encouraging. The English Jacobites once again reiterated their refusal to rise without foreign intervention. Since France was out of the question (despite continued Jacobite sympathies among some very high-ranking French ministers), Charles had no choice but to find an alternative great-power sponsor. Negotiations for a marriage between the Jacobite prince and the Duke of Daremberg's daughter, who would bring a dowry of 12,000 troops, proved abortive, and, *faute de mieux*, Charles turned to Frederick.[91]

Frederick's agenda in his contacts with the Jacobites, which included a personal interview with Charles Edward and entertaining a proposal for a marriage between the Jacobite prince and his daughter, is obscure, but certain lines of interest seem to stand out more than others. Frederick was apprehensive about the Duke of Newcastle's attempts to have Maria-Theresa's son Joseph elected King of the Romans (i.e. heir apparent to the Holy Roman Empire), lest this prove the basis of an Anglo-Austrian rapprochement whose culmination would be the recovery of Silesia from Prussia by the Habsburgs.[92] More importantly, Frederick wanted to mend his fences with France, Prussia's ally during the War of the Austrian Succession. By the time the war ended in 1748, Frederick's diplomatic tergiversations had thoroughly alienated Louis XV and his ministers – leaving Frederick uncomfortably isolated in the face of the Habsburgs' manifest thirst for revenge.[93] Frederick, like Peter the Great before him, believed Jacobite influence in France could work in his favour, and therefore posed as a potential ally to the Jacobites to get in their (and ultimately France's) good graces.

Charles Edward quickly perceived Frederick's fundamental indifference to the Jacobite cause, but found himself locked into a 'partnership' with him because of the English Jacobites' insistence on outside support and their deference towards the Earl Marischal, whom Frederick had astutely appointed his ambassador to Paris in 1751.[94] Marischal was absolutely Frederick's man by this time, but the British government and the English Jacobites were both ignorant of the fact, and responded exactly as Frederick desired. The Pelham ministry was alarmed at the appointment of such a notorious 'Jacobite', and reacted first by stepping up their surveillance of Jacobite activity and then by seeking ways to conciliate Frederick.[95] The English Jacobites meanwhile obsequiously accorded Marischal a virtual veto on any uprising, and by insisting that he be present at all meetings to discuss and plan the projected rebellion, made sure that Frederick was perfectly informed as to when he should instruct Marischal to use it.

Charles Edward understood very well what Frederick was about, and tried to manoeuvre and coax the English Jacobites into rebelling in any case, but found himself blocked at every turn by Marischal. He was not helped in his endeavours by the transparent desperation of the plans for a rising, which centred on seizing the Hanoverian royal family and whisking them off to confinement in France, or else holding them hostage until reinforcements arrived. Alexander Murray of Elibank, the main liaison between Charles and the plotters (from which the conspiracy derived the name by which it is usually known: the 'Elibank' plot), finally killed it at the English end when he realised that there was no hope of Prussian or French aid and that the English Jacobites were being manoeuvred into going it alone. By then, however, Charles had already sent two trusted agents from the Scottish exiled community, Donald Macdonell of Lochgarry and Dr Archibald Cameron, to Scotland to prepare the clans and spread the news of the Jacobite prince's conversion to Anglicanism. A spy in Charles Edward's entourage (Aleistair Ruadh Macdonell of Glengarry) passed on an exact account of the agents' itinerary to his paymasters. Cameron was arrested and Lochgarry barely escaped. Though Cameron refused to talk, the Scots Jacobites prudently went to ground, effectively ending the plot, though Frederick toyed with the English Jacobites for a little longer.[96]

Charles responded to the plot's failure in what was by now his usual fashion: shrill denunciations of his erstwhile comrades for cowardice and treachery, chronic drunkenness and brutality towards his mistress of the moment. The unfortunate lady in question at the time of the collapse of the Elibank plot was Clementina Walkinshaw, subsequently the mother of Charles's only child, Charlotte. She was also wrongly believed to be a Hanoverian spy by the English Jacobites. They had accordingly requested that Charles Edward send her away when she renewed their former liaison (she had become his mistress in Scotland in 1746) at Ghent in 1752. Charles refused, so when Cameron was arrested – clearly on exact information from an informer – the English Jacobites assumed it was Clementina who had betrayed him. Disgusted with his alcoholic petulance and refusal even to hear their advice, the English Jacobites began to distance themselves from him. Finally, in a boozy fit of pique during a dispute with Marischal and the English conspirators in 1754, Charles appears to have threatened to publish the names of the Elibank plotters for having 'betrayed' him (see document 8).[97] This was truly the death-knell of the Jacobite cause. The handful of elite Jacobites who knew no better might still toast 'Bonnie Prince Charlie' at commemorative dinners, and the poor, ignorant clansmen might still cherish his name in song and story, but the paranoid, sodden, brutal reality was too much to bear and certainly not worth risking one's life for.[98]

The Papacy

Since the exiled Stuarts' claim that, 'professing the Roman Catholick religion was the only [occasion] that actually did or possibly could make us lose our crown', was manifestly true, it would seem reasonable to assume that the attitude of the Holy See towards James II and his heirs would be warmly supportive.[99] In fact, for some time after the Revolution there was little correspondence between the Stuarts' sufferings in the cause of Catholicism and the Vatican's regard for them.

This frigidity was principally occasioned by the close ties between St Germain and Versailles. Pope Alexander VIII and his successor Innocent XII were bitterly opposed to Louis XIV's imperialism, which was as aggressive inside as outside the church, and their hostility to the French king spilled over into their attitude toward James II, whom the Holy See (not without cause) regarded as simply a client of the Sun-King.[100] Furthermore, although the nuances of the relationship between the papacy and the Stuarts were not apparent to most British Protestants, their aims and objectives were not necessarily the same. The Stuarts aimed at a second restoration, after which they could further the Counter-Reformation in Britain. The Holy See's main objective was the survival of the underground Catholic churches in the three kingdoms. It was not necessarily the case that this end would best be served by intriguing on behalf of, and subsidising, the exiled Stuarts. The papacy was, furthermore, aligned diplomatically with the Austrian and Spanish Habsburgs, who were both in turn allies of William III. Neither of these powers favoured a Stuart restoration in the 1690s either, but both sympathised with their co-religionists in the British Isles. Thus by withholding support for James II the Vatican could hope in the long term to persuade the Revolutionary regime in the British Isles to wink at the continued operation of the Catholic church there, and if in the event religious animus overcame the inclination to let sleeping dogs lie, invoke the intercession of Britain's Catholic allies. Consequently James II's emissaries were accorded the minimum access protocol and piety would allow, and his petitions and appeals for support were ignored.

Relations between St Germain and the Vatican improved in the late 1690s in line with Louis XIV and Innocent XII's pragmatic settlement of the Gallican dispute, and by the time of James

II's death in 1701 they were sufficiently warm for Clement XI
to intercede with Louis to ask that he recognise the Old Pretender
as James 'III'.[101] The increasingly *dévot*, if somewhat Jansenist,
inclinations of the Stuart royal family further facilitated the gathering rapprochement between the two courts, and by 1713, when
the Old Pretender was forced to leave France for Lorraine, he was
already in receipt of a small but useful papal pension and was close
to being granted the right of nomination to Catholic bishophrics
in the British Isles.[102] Yet despite the real improvement in their
relationship, James and Clement were both careful to keep their
overt contacts to a formal minimum. The Old Pretender did not
want to alarm and offend his erstwhile Protestant subjects by
being seen to be deferential to the papacy.[103] Clement XI (and
his successors) did not want the port of Rome at Civitavecchia
to receive a martial visit from the Royal Navy or the retaliatory
enforcement of the penal laws against the British Catholic community. Hence James was very loth to take refuge in the Papal
States, and the Holy See wished to avoid the necessity of having
to offer him asylum.

Their wishes on the matter proved of little consequence, however, in the face of British determination to force the Old Pretender
into close and visible association with the papacy. The most
effective propaganda against the exiled Stuarts always centred
on their Catholicism. Therefore forcing the Old Pretender and
his followers into closer physical proximity to the pope was well
calculated to associate the Stuarts and the Scarlet Whore of Rome
in the minds of most of their erstwhile subjects. In 1716 British
diplomatic pressure on James's host, the Duke of Lorraine, duly
obliged him to quit Lorraine for Avignon, a papal enclave in
southern France. That would not do either, and in 1717 British
threats to bombard Civitavecchia and French hints that British
pressure might force them to invade Avignon unless Clement
persuaded James to move on to Italy produced the desired result.
After a brief, unhappy interlude at Urbino, the Jacobite court finally
settled at Rome in 1719.[104]

Rome was at least a comfortable, civilised place of exile. The
ageing Pope Clement was no longer especially enthusiastic about
the Jacobite cause, but he treated the exiled Stuarts very hospitably.
The fruits of his generosity: the Palazzo Muti in Rome, a villa at
Albano and the substantial pension he allowed the Old Pretender,

were a vital injection of material support at a time when the Stuart cause was languishing. Moreover, he allowed James's Protestant followers to conduct private religious services (something they were never officially allowed throughout their period in France) and did what he could to shield the Jacobite community from harassment by British spies.[105] Perhaps just as importantly from the point of view of the exiled court's morale, he and his successors continued to accord the Stuarts full royal honours up to the death of James 'III' in 1766. During that period too occasional extraordinary subventions (such as the substantial sums Benedict XIV contributed during the '45) and fairly constant diplomatic support combined to help keep the Jacobite cause afloat.[106]

There was, however, a negative aspect to the papacy's kindness and generosity. He who pays the piper (and even more so he who houses him) may call the tune, and the papacy in like manner expected the exiled Stuarts to uphold the Catholic cause as interpreted by the papal administration of the day. In the event of a Stuart restoration the papacy's expectations would doubtless have centred on the achievement of concrete legal protection for the Catholic minority.[107] Since this never arose, its influence was exercised on the moral tone and personnel of the Stuart court instead. Hence the papacy's ill-judged involvement in the running dispute between James and his wife, Clementina Sobieska, over the tutors appointed to oversee the education of the Jacobite princes and whether or not Lady Hay (the wife of Jacobite Secretary of State John Hay of Cromlix), whom James wanted to appoint one of the 'Queen's' ladies-in-waiting, was James's mistress. Heartened by Pope Benedict XIII's investigation of her husband's moral probity and whether or not Protestant tutors might prove a bad influence on the Jacobite princes, Clementina held out for the Hays' dismissal and ultimately achieved her end – thereby sullying James's reputation for religious tolerance in Britain. Even Clement XII's refusal to continue to support her, which forced her to submit to James, could not clear the imputation that the Old Pretender was hen-pecked and 'priest-ridden', and the gathering consensus among the British Jacobites that James should abdicate in favour of Charles Edward, which first arose during the 1730s, may be more than temporally related to this perception of the Old Pretender.[108]

There was a negative aspect to the relationship between the

Jacobite court and the Holy See from the church's point of view too. James 'III' was always a good son of the church, orthodox (apart from some apparent sympathy with Jansenism) in all his practices, who always showed a proper respect for the papacy. His younger son, Henry Benedict, the 'Duke of York', likewise showed exemplary piety from an early age, and in 1747, as has been mentioned, fled from his older brother's bullying in France back to Italy to be first ordained and then rapidly promoted to cardinal (all with his father's connivance).[109] Charles Edward took a very different attitude to Catholicism, and beyond it to the Holy See. The prince's latest biographer advances a cogent case for his being a religious sceptic of the 'couldn't care less' variety. The upshot was that Charles Edward cynically squeezed misguidedly reverential Catholic churchmen for every penny he could get, as for example during his sojourn in Avignon in 1748–9 where he ran up huge debts for the papal administration to settle after his departure. The prince's singularly ill-judged conversion to Anglicanism in 1750 stemmed from the same stock of indifference to the religious sensibilities of contemporary Europe, which despite the much-lauded exploits of the French *philosophes* remained a pious, observant society on both sides of the religious divide.[110] In all this shabbiness, capped in the 1760s by Charles's return to Catholicism after the English Jacobites stopped sending him sufficient funds to keep him in the lifestyle to which he wanted to become accustomed, it was the Catholic church and the papacy in particular that had to pick up the bill and clear up the mess. Consequently, though there were good diplomatic reasons, to do with serving the best interests of the British Catholic community, for Pope Clement XIII's refusal to recognise Charles as king on his father's death in 1766, disgust at the prince's behaviour since 1746 may well have ensured the decision was easy to make.[111]

Despite this formal repudiation of the Stuarts the papacy quietly continued to look after the last members of the family. Papal subventions helped sustain Charles Edward up until his death in 1788, and it was primarily the papacy that cleared up the mess (again) after his wife, Louise of Stolberg, fled his alcoholic violence in 1780 for the superior charms of her lover, Count Alfieri (see document 9).[112] In the same vein, Cardinal Henry Benedict Stuart received the rich benefice of Frascati and was promoted first to Vice-Chancellor of the Holy See and subsequently Dean of the Sacred College. Moreover Pope Pius VI, though he never formally recognised Henry as king, nonetheless encouraged him to adopt the royal arms and title. Henry 'IX' duly enjoyed the attendant empty pomp and circumstance until he was forced to flee the armies of Revolutionary France in 1798. Ironically, the first time Henry ever set foot on British territory was when the British government sent a warship to evacuate him and assorted other papal dignitaries to Sicily before they were overrun by the Jacobin hordes. Finding him destitute in Venice a year later, a British agent there arranged for a pension of £5,000 to be paid to the old man, courtesy of George III. Allowed to resume his see and offices after Napoleon's concordat with Pope Pius VII, he died back in Frascati in 1807.[113] It is perhaps fitting that the last scion of the 'unlucky race' of Stuarts who lost their throne for their commitment to the Catholic church should have died so firmly nestling in its bosom.

Notes

1 H. T. Dickinson, *Bolingbroke*, 1970, pp. 140–2.

2 Gregg, 'Jacobite career of John, Earl of Mar', pp. 183–4.

3 *Lockhart Papers*, II, p. 405.

4 Plumb, *Political Stability*, pp. 187–9; Colley, *Britons*, pp. 71–85, 376–7; J. Rule, *Albion's People. English Society, 1714–1815*, 1992, p. 167.

5 See for example, Bennett, *Tory Crisis*, pp. 207–9; Cruickshanks, *Political Untouchables*, p. 42.

6 Fritz, *English Ministers and Jacobitism*, pp. 51–8, 109–25; D. Szechi, ed., *Letters of George Lockhart of Carnwath, 1698–1732*, Scottish History Society, 1989, pp. 316–17.

7 J. Black, *Eighteenth Century Europe 1700–1789*, New York, 1990, p. 278.

8 For this and much of what follows below see G. Parker, *The Military Revolution. Military Innovation and the Rise of the West, 1500–1800*, 1988; D. Chandler, *The Art of Warfare in the Age of Marlborough*, 1976; and Duffy, *Military Experience*.

9 Fritz, *English Ministers and Jacobitism*, pp. 20–1, 54.

10 Michael, *Beginnings of the Hanoverian Dynasty*, pp. 150–3, 202–3, 312–17, 326–7.

11 A. M. Wilson, *French Foreign Policy During the Administration of Cardinal Fleury 1726–1743. A Study in Diplomacy and Commercial Development*, Westport, Connecticutt, repr. 1972, pp. 17–20.

12 Bennett, *Tory Crisis*, pp. 233–6, 238–9, 246.

13 Fritz, *English Ministers and Jacobitism*, pp. 73–6.

14 Paul Monod interprets the fragments that survive of the plan differently than the above, which is based on Fritz's analysis. According to Monod (private communication to the author, 12 February 1993), the first stage was to be a series of disturbances in the constituencies, followed by a riot in London. This was to be used as cover for a military coup led by Tory army officers. When the Irish landed they were to be joined by the Waltham 'Blacks' (i.e. gangs of poachers/smugglers) led by Sir Harry Goring, and march on London.

15 Bennett, *Tory Crisis*, pp. 245–9; Gregg, 'John, Earl of Mar', pp. 189–90.

16 Fritz, *English Ministers and Jacobitism*, pp. 82–96.

17 E. Cruickshanks, 'Lord Cornbury, Bolingbroke and a plan to restore the Stuarts, 1731–1735', *Royal Stuart Papers*, XXVII, 1986, pp. 4–5.

18 Wilson, *French Foreign Policy*, pp. 230–1.

19 Stuart Papers 162/165: Colonel Daniel O'Brien to the Old Pretender, Paris, 25 June 1733 ns.

20 Cruickshanks, 'Lord Cornbury', pp. 5–9.

21 Wilson, *French Foreign Policy*, pp. 324–6.

22 W. B. Blaikie, ed., *Origins of the Forty-Five and Other Papers Relating to That Rising*, Edinburgh, repr. 1975, xxvi–xl.

23 Cruickshanks, *Political Untouchables*, pp. 25–9. Cf. Colley, *In Defiance*, pp. 226–35, 239–42.

24 Cruickshanks, *Political Untouchables*, pp. 38–50.

25 Ibid., pp. 52–64. Cf. McLynn, *Charles Edward Stuart*, pp. 88–93.

26 Ibid., pp. 94–111.

27 Ibid., pp. 111–22. Cf. Lenman, *Jacobite Risings*, pp. 241–3.

28 McLynn, *Charles Edward Stuart*, pp. 127–8.

29 Lenman, *Jacobite Risings*, p. 248.

30 McLynn, *Charles Edward Stuart*, pp. 129–40.

31 K. Tomasson and F. Buist, *Battles of the '45*, repr. 1978, pp. 31–65.

32 McLynn, *France and the '45*, p. 75.

33 Ibid., pp. 61–2.

34 McLynn, *Charles Edward Stuart*, pp. 132–3.

35 McLynn, *France and the '45*, pp. 75–98, 102.

36 F. J. McLynn, *The Jacobite Army in England, 1745. The Final Campaign*, Edinburgh, 1983, pp. 8–10.

37 Ibid., p. 197.

38 McLynn, *Charles Edward Stuart*, pp. 183–8.

39 McLynn, *Jacobite Army in England*, pp. 116–23, 130–1.

40 McLynn, *France and the '45*, pp. 119–39.

41 Sedgwick, *House of Commons*, I, pp. 74–5.

42 E. Charteris, ed., *A Short Account of the Affairs of Scotland in the Years*

1744, 1745, 1746, by David, Lord Elcho, Edinburgh, 1907, pp. 294–5, 301–2, 303–4, 310, 328, 337–40, 413.

43 The interpretation above is based on, but differs with, Dr McLynn's meticulously researched reconstruction of the council at Derby, for which see: *Jacobite Army in England*, pp. 125–9.

44 McLynn, *Charles Edward Stuart*, pp. 196–200.

45 McLynn, *Jacobite Army in England*, pp. 136–94 *passim*.

46 McLynn, *France and the '45*, pp. 147–55, 159–60, 174–8, 180.

47 Tomasson and Buist, *Battles of the '45* pp. 95–112.

48 Cf. McLynn, *Charles Edward Stuart*, pp. 201, 203–4, 210, 211–12, 214–17.

49 Tomasson and Buist, *Battles of the '45*, pp. 117–78 *passim*.

50 McLynn, *Charles Edward Stuart*, pp. 261–3.

51 Ibid., pp. 265–324.

52 Ibid., pp. 350–68.

53 Ibid., pp. 327–32, 369–447 *passim*.

54 C. Nordmann, 'Choiseul and the last Jacobite attempt of 1759', in Cruickshanks, *Ideology and Conspiracy*, pp. 201–10.

55 McLynn, *Charles Edward Stuart*, pp. 492–500.

56 Hatton, *George I*, pp. 184–6.

57 R. M. Hatton, *Charles XII of Sweden*, New York, 1968, pp. 62, 366, 369–70, 398, 403–4.

58 Michael, *Beginnings of the Hanoverian Dynasty*, pp. 290–2, 297–302.

59 Hatton, *Charles XII*, p. 445.

60 Fritz, *English Ministers and Jacobitism*, pp. 9–10.

61 Ibid., pp. 12–14.

62 Hatton, *Charles XII*, pp. 416–17, 425, 438.

63 Fritz, *English Ministers and Jacobitism*, pp. 14–18.

64 Ibid., pp. 21–2, 23–4, 27.

65 Hatton, *Charles XII*, p. 449.

66 Sedgwick, *House of Commons*, I, p. 514.

67 C. Gill, 'The affair of Porto Novo: an incident in Anglo-Swedish relations', *English Historical Review*, LXXIII, 1958, p. 60; G. Behre, 'Sweden and the rising of 1745', *Scottish Historical Review*, LI, 1972, pp. 148–71.

68 McLynn, *Charles Edward Stuart*, pp. 530–6.

69 M. S. Anderson, *Europe in the Eighteenth Century 1713/1783*, repr. 1970, pp. 217–18.

70 S. Harcourt-Smith, *Alberoni, or the Spanish Conspiracy*, 1943, pp. 113–17.

71 L. B. Smith, 'Spain and the Jacobites, 1715–16', in Cruickshanks, *Ideology and Conspiracy*, pp. 162–71.

72 L. B. Smith, *Spain and Britain 1715–1719. The Jacobite Issue*, 1987, pp. 82–91.

73 Michael, *Beginnings of the Hanoverian Dynasty*, pp. 355–8.

74 Haile, *James Francis Edward*, p. 263; Smith, *Spain and Britain*, pp. 163–82.

75 Smith, *Spain and Britain*, pp. 164–5, 176–7, 183, 195–7.

76 Michael, *Quadruple Alliance*, pp. 189–92; Lenman, *Jacobite Risings*, p. 190.

77 Smith, *Spain and Britain*, pp. 198–9.

78 Ibid., pp. 210–23.

79 Michael, *Quadruple Alliance*, pp. 99–115, 119–20, 125–6.

80 McLynn, *Charles Edward Stuart*, pp. 16–20; Haile, *James Francis Edward*, pp. 312–25.

81 McLynn, *Charles Edward Stuart*, pp. 319–22.

82 Michael, *Beginnings of the Hanoverian Dynasty*, pp. 286–7.

83 D. McKay, 'The struggle for control of George I's northern policy, 1718–19', *Journal of Modern History*, XLV, 1973, pp. 367–71; Black, *Eighteenth Century*, p. 286.

84 Jones, *Main-Stream*, pp. 132–3, 142; M. W. Bruce, 'Jacobite relations with Peter the Great', *Slavonic Review*, XIV, 1935–6, pp. 346–7.

85 Ibid., pp. 345–61.

86 McLynn, *Charles Edward Stuart*, pp. 33, 324.

87 *Pace* his authorship of a tract entitled *Anti-Machiavel*.

88 Anderson, *Europe in the Eighteenth Century*, pp. 201–4.

89 McLynn, *Charles Edward Stuart*, p. 308.

90 Ibid., pp. 401–2.

91 Ibid., pp. 396–400.

92 P. Langford, *The Eighteenth Century 1688–1815*, 1976, pp. 131–2.

93 Anderson, *Europe in the Eighteenth Century*, pp. 207–9.

94 McLynn, *Charles Edward Stuart*, pp. 402–3.

95 D. B. Horn, *Great Britain and Europe in the Eighteenth Century*, Oxford, 1967, pp. 154–5.

96 McLynn, *Charles Edward Stuart*, pp. 403–11.

97 *Affairs of Scotland*, pp. 148–9 (see below, p. 151). Cf. McLynn, *Charles Edward Stuart*, pp. 392–3, 406, 421–31.

98 Ibid., pp. 435, 436–7, 440–1, 447, 451, 455.

99 Carte MS 181, f. 611r: instructions for the Duke of Perth's embassy to Rome, (St Germain) 7 March 1695 ns.

100 Bluche, *Louis XIV*, pp. 303–6; Blairs Letters 1/131/14: Walter Leslie to L. Leslie, Rome, 31 January 1690 ns; *Original Papers*, I, pp. 532–4: Perth to Caryll, Rome, 6 and 7 June 1695 ns.

101 Bluche, *Louis XIV*, p. 521.

102 Haile, *James Francis Edward*, pp. 115–16, 135; Szechi, *Jacobitism and Tory Politics*, p. 11; *Eighteenth-Century Ireland*, p. 91.

103 Jones, *Main-Stream*, p. 125.

104 Michael, *Beginnings of the Hanoverian Dynasty*, p. 203; F. J. McLynn, *The Jacobites*, 1985, p. 162; Haile, *James Francis Edward*, pp. 230–1, 244, 277.

105 McLynn, *Jacobites*, pp. 163–4, 180–1.

106 McLynn, *Charles Edward Stuart*, pp. 71, 123, 166, 275.

107 Ibid., p. 166.

108 McLynn, *Charles Edward Stuart*, p. 43; Haile, *James Francis Edward*, pp. 311–19, 336–8, 400.

109 McLynn, *Jacobites*, pp. 165, 204; *Charles Edward Stuart*, pp. 327–31.

110 Ibid., pp. 348–9, 371–6, 399.

111 Ibid., pp. 468–77.

112 Ibid., pp. 516–17, 523–5, 526–30, 536.

113 Petrie, *Jacobite Movement*, pp. 271–6.

5

The Jacobite diaspora,
1688–1788

The term 'diaspora' is used in the title of this chapter deliberately to evoke a comparison. The original diaspora was created by the expulsion of the Jews from their Holy Land into exile among the Gentiles, there to await a messiah who would lead them home. Hence it is an appropriate term to describe what happened to the Jacobites in the century after 1688. They too lost their homeland to infidels, and they too languished in exile awaiting a redeemer. For the Jacobites, however, there were two forms of diaspora, one material, the other spiritual. Those who fled to the Continent in 1688–9 and after were physically cut off from their roots and formed a visible community of exiles. Those who remained in the British Isles ultimately experienced a diaspora too, but of the spiritual variety, when the cause disintegrated in the 1750s. Former Jacobites were left adrift in the wash and eddy of late-eighteenth-century politics, and they, like their counterparts overseas, had to adapt themselves once more to living among people who neither knew nor cared for the cause they had cherished for so long. This chapter accordingly deals with the diaspora in two parts. The first part looks at the Jacobite exiles in Europe, the second at what became of the Jacobites in Britain and Ireland.

The external diaspora

The Jacobite community in Europe was, by and large, a patrician phenomenon. A good number of Irish plebeians marched off to exile in France when the garrison of Limerick was offered the alternative of exile or surrender in 1691, but this was one of very few instances of substantial numbers of plebeian Jacobites fleeing overseas. They had neither the sophistication nor the means to be able independently to make new lives for themselves in alien climes, and consequently the few plebeian Jacobites who fetched up on the Continent were virtually all soldiers or servants. The French and Spanish armies continued to recruit surreptitiously in Ireland throughout the Jacobite period, and exiled Scottish regiments were organised in France and Sweden, so there was always a plebeian presence in the European Jacobite diaspora, but it was a transient epiphenomenon. Despite the trickle of recruits from the British Isles (principally Ireland), the 'Wild Geese' regiments rapidly integrated into the larger society they were serving. Most of the rank-and-file were, or soon became, Catholics, married local women and settled into a new life overseas. By the time of the '45 the common soldiers of the formerly Jacobite regiments who were slipped into Scotland to assist Charles Edward were mostly French-speaking and second or third generation French subjects, for all that they sported names like Kelly, Burke and Macdonald.[1]

Their patrician counterparts' experience of exile was more varied and painful. Though one should never underrate the ties of home, it probably hurt more to leave broad acres, a fine house and a pleasant, comfortable lifestyle, as the stereotypical patrician Jacobite did, than the unremitting toil and near-poverty that characterised much of plebeian rural life in the British Isles. On the other hand, patrician Jacobites' social status did ease their reception in Europe. The European social elite in large part shared a common culture in the eighteenth century. French fashions, mores and tastes dominated high society almost everywhere, and patrician Jacobites arriving from the British Isles consequently found much that was familiar in their new environment. Moreover, the tradition of elite hospitality to 'distressed gentlefolk', which the patrician Jacobites manifestly were, initially assured most of them of food and shelter at the very least.[2] Thereafter, however, the paths and problems of the various categories of patrician Jacobites diverge.

Patrician Catholic Jacobites were enormously helped in adapting to life on the Continent by pre-existing networks long since established by their co-religionists. Irish religious communities and seminaries already existed in Paris, Rome, Brussels and Madrid (to name only the most important), and the Scots Colleges in Paris and Rome dated back to the sixteenth century. They were accordingly able to ease the transition of their Catholic fellow-countrymen by extending charity to them and helping them make the right connexions with the local elites if they needed commissions in the armed forces or financial succour from the local authorities. As well, Catholic Irish merchants had for a long time been using the sympathy and easier access their religion vouchsafed to facilitate their trade with France, the Low Countries and Spain.[3] As a consequence, long before the Jacobite exiles arrived there were already small, prosperous communities of Irish expatriates in many of the major trading ports of the French and Spanish western seaboards. These communities too could and did provide charity and access to sympathetic officials, which helped ease the path of those Catholic patricians, men like Robert Gordon and Aeneas Macdonald, who sought to make a new career for themselves in commerce.[4]

Above and beyond the existing support networks provided by established Scots and Irish Catholic expatriate communities, it was in any case easier for patrician Catholic Jacobites to adapt to life on the Continent because of the social environment in those countries where Jacobites were most welcome. The majority of Jacobite exiles settled in France, Italy and Spain (in that order) – three of the most intensely Catholic countries in Europe. The Catholic church in these countries never sought to persecute the exiled Protestant Jacobite community, but there was some friction, for example over the obstinate refusal of Louis XIV to allow Protestant services at St Germain and the equally obdurate refusal of the Parisian church authorities to allow the Protestants a graveyard in which to bury their dead.[5] Thus, whereas the Catholics fitted in quite easily, over the course of time such rubs irritated the exiled Protestants. Moreover, because the British and Irish Catholic communities had for some time been sending their children to the Continent to be educated in a suitably Roman Catholic fashion, a high proportion of the Catholic exiles must have already been familiar with French or Spanish mores and thus found it easier to settle down in their new home. The Protestant exiles found themselves in a more alien environment than their Catholic counterparts. Certainly, of all the categories of patrician exiles, the most likely to despair and seek, often desperately, to return home, were the Protestants.[6]

There was, of course, a way out of the problem: conversion to Roman Catholicism. And in order to take up commissions in the French and Spanish armies, make themselves eligible to marry aristocratic French and Spanish brides, or simply the better to get on with their new lives in France or Italy, many patrician Protestant exiles did conform to the Catholic church.[7] By doing so they handed every post-Revolutionary regime a surfeit of black propaganda, and from 1689 onwards every regime that had cause to fear the Jacobites made ample use of this natural drift towards Catholicism among the exiled community.[8] A handful of senior Jacobites, such as the Duke of Ormond and the Earl Marischal, were both sufficiently stubborn and sufficiently eminent to be able to hold out for commissions in the Spanish and French armies without compromising their religious integrity (and the requirement that all French officers be Catholics was too increasingly relaxed as the eighteenth century wore on), but the majority of patrician Protestants were therefore left economically dependent on whatever they had carried into exile with them and occasional remittances from home. No better recipe for penurious frustration could have been devised, which may go some way toward explaining the backbiting, paranoia and religious jealousy that seems to have characterised the Jacobite diaspora in Europe.[9]

Nevertheless, taken in the round, the Jacobites' contribution to their host societies was out of all proportion to their numbers. It was primarily military because that was the only marketable skill most Jacobites possessed, but nonetheless important for all that. Admiral Thomas Gordon, for example, who was recruited by Peter the Great after he was dismissed from the Royal Navy for political unreliability in 1715, was the tsar's executive arm in the creation of a modern, formidable navy. Peter Lacy served his Russian employer so well he was promoted to field-marshal and made governor of Livonia.[10] James Fitzjames, Duke of Berwick, was the architect of the Bourbon victory in Spain during the War of Spanish Succession. The only general the Hapsburg empire ever found who could fight Frederick the Great to a standstill was the Irish exile Maximilian Ulysses Browne. On the other side of the lines James Keith died heroically trying to save the Prussian army at Hochkirk, while his brother Marischal, as we have seen, became Frederick's trusted agent and ambassador as well as general.[11] And though remarkable military careers were the main legacy of the Jacobite diaspora, a number of Jacobites made very significant contributions elsewhere. The Walsh family, who made a fortune as privateers-cum-merchants, typify the vigour and aggression which the scattering of Jacobite commercial dynasties added to the commercial life of France's burgeoning western seaboard towns. The Swedish East India Company was largely founded and run by the Scottish exile community in Gothenburg. Though it collapsed in a financial panic in 1720, Controller-General of Finances John Law's Mississippi scheme bid fair to retrieve the *ancien régime* in France from the permanent state of incipient bankruptcy that was eventually to bring it down in 1789. Bankers like Aeneas Macdonald and John Waters were active agents in modernising France's financial sector. John Holker almost single-handedly created a modern textile industry in France, and was ennobled for his efforts.[12] All in all, there can be no doubt that a lot of talent left the British Isles as a result of the failures of the Jacobite cause, and it served its new European masters well.

The internal diaspora

In England the Jacobite community effectively lost its faith in the mid-1750s. Disgust with Charles Edward, and despair at the lack of any realistic prospect of ever overcoming the military might of the Whig ascendancy mounted to the point where the Tories became permanently detached from the inner, Nonjuring and Catholic, core of the cause. Ironically, this seems to have finally demoralised the party, so that when William Pitt the Elder began to espouse traditional Tory 'patriotic' policies they rapidly became his poodles.[13] The party maintained a truncated existence a while longer before finally disintegrating in the aftermath of their readmission to court and public office by the utterly respectable, thoroughly English and Anglican George III.[14] Within the inner core of the Jacobite cause, the Nonjurors were badly hurt by their participation in the '45, and thereafter their numbers seem to have steadily diminished. The patrician families whose benefactions and protection had sustained them drifted back into conformity with the Church of England, and the Nonjuring community gradually wasted away. The last known Nonjuring service was in Manchester in 1804. Some of the Catholics stayed loyal to Charles Edward throughout the remainder of his miserable life, but from 1766 he was no longer formally recognised as 'King of England' by the papacy, and their respect for him and remittances to him waned with the passing of the older generation.[15]

The final destination, in political terms, of the English Jacobites and their connexions after the disintegration of the Jacobite cause is often obscure, but in the few cases where we can trace their path back into constitutional politics it is as varied as the individuals themselves. Peter Legh, for example, scion of a Nonjuring dynasty who sat in Parliament for his family's pocket borough of Newton in succession to the Jacobites' Parliamentary leader, Will Shippen, by 1764 was featuring in a list of 'sure friends' drawn up by the Whig Duke of Newcastle.[16] John Pugh Pryse, a descendant of Lewis Pryse (a leading Welsh Jacobite), and a former member of the Jacobite Sea-Serjeants club himself, by contrast was a keen supporter of John Wilkes.[17] The Earl of Westmoreland took a still different route when, after nearly two decades of Jacobite plotting, he attended George III's coronation, kissed the king's hand and was promoted to general in the army.[18] The overall pattern of the transition can only be tentatively assessed, but it would nonetheless appear that despite the fact that former Jacobites were to be found among all the factions and parties of late-eighteenth-century politics, there *may* have been a tendency for them to accumulate at the radical end of the spectrum. If this was the case, it is not in itself surprising. Jacobites and radicals both yearned for a return to the good old days of sturdy yeomen and good masters, and neither was enamoured with the Hanoverian dynasty and its corrupt Whig handmaidens (see document 7). Ex-Jacobites, like ex-Chartists in the nineteenth century, may thus have acted as conduits for the transmission of a tradition of resistance to the established order and as well transmitted to their posterity an abiding sense of its illegitimacy. Thus as one recent writer on the subject has put it: 'The roses of 10 June [the Old Pretender's birthday] had withered to ashes by the time the English working class was born; but their sweet aroma may have wafted around the cradle.'[19]

Jacobites north of the border suffered the same tendency to disillusionment with Charles Edward and the prospect of eventual victory over the Whig regime as their English counterparts, but reinforced in spates by their experiences in 1745–6. In retrospect it was all too apparent that Charles Edward had deliberately misled them, and that his refusal to fight on after Culloden had condemned them to condign punishment when a guerrilla war (at which the clans were past masters) might have extracted a negotiated peace. While they were lying low after 1746 they had, moreover, plenty of leisure to contemplate the consequences of their failure, as they watched the Highlands being brutally harried by the Duke of Cumberland's forces, the clan system fatally undermined by the confiscation of estates and the abolition of heritable jurisdictions (in flat contravention of the treaty of Union) and Episcopalian clergymen vigorously persecuted.[20] This period of reflection seems to have generated an urge among a good number of former Jacobites to reach some form of *modus vivendi* with the Whig regime. When the opportunity to do so arose in the mid-1750s first a few, then steadily more and more, patrician Scottish Jacobites seized it.

The 'way back' to legitimacy in Scotland was pioneered by Simon Fraser, Master of Lovat, whose father Lord Lovat was executed for treason in 1747 and who was himself 'out' in the '45, and it took the form of raising his clan to fight the Hanoverian dynasty's wars overseas. This was, of course, nicely dressed up in the appropriate forms. Technically Fraser was simply given a commission to raise a regiment for service in the Seven Years War. Back in Scotland, however, he raised that regiment by unofficially mobilising the clan's Tacksmen to produce their manrent in the traditional fashion. His clansmen then marched off to die heroically in America. By the end of the war General Simon Fraser was once again an accepted, respectable member of Hanoverian high society, and his fellow chieftains were eager to follow his lead.[21] During the American Revolution they got the chance to do so, and one after another all the major clans (and some of the minor ones) dutifully provided cannon-fodder sufficient to ease their chieftains' passage back into the good graces of the government.[22] The seal was put on the former Jacobites' reconciliation with the Whig establishment by legislation passed in 1784 returning to their former owners estates confiscated in 1746 that had not already been surreptitiously reacquired by them. By the time the Episcopalian church formally ceased to pray for the exiled Stuarts in its services – when Charles Edward died in 1788 – there was already nothing left of the Jacobite cause in Scotland but sad songs and fine poetry.

On the surface Ireland was virtually free of Jacobites and Jacobitism from 1691 onwards. *De facto*, in the 'hidden' Ireland of
secretive Catholic peasants and isolated Gaelic-speaking villages
it of course continued to flourish. Among plebeian Catholics tales
of redeeming heroes were insensibly adapted to feature the Old
Pretender and Charles Edward (the bards and storytellers never
forgave James II for his precipitous flight after the battle of the
Boyne), while the dwindling band of patrician Catholics sought
solace in some hauntingly beautiful (*aisling*) poetry recalling their
former glory, and by implication hoping the returning Stuarts
would restore it.[23] As late as the 1760s the Whiteboys were
still taking secret oaths that pledged them to fight for a Stuart
restoration.[24] This underground culture was naturally resistant to
the forces of change, disillusionment and despair that destroyed
Jacobitism elsewhere in the British Isles, and consequently may
have lingered into the 1790s. Hence the oaths and rhetoric of
the Defenders (plebeian Catholic secret society that succeeded the
Whiteboys) who were recruited to fight for Ireland's freedom by
republican, Protestant, United Irishmen between 1796 and 1798 still
contained references to the Stuarts.[25] Ireland's peculiar brand of
sectarian oppression was, nevertheless, clearly already giving rise
to enduring patterns of resentment and resistance that would make
its social and political development unique within the British Isles.
The hidden Ireland's lingering affection for the Jacobite cause was
a symptom rather than a cause of this. Hence the transition from
monarchism to republicanism as the guiding light of this secret
culture that took place at the end of the eighteenth century was
relatively easy; both were means to an end – the overthrow of the
ruling elite.

Jacobitism came to an end in each kingdom when the inner core
who had sheltered and nurtured it finally abandoned the cause.
In England and Scotland it stemmed from defeat and disillusion,
and ended in reconciliation with the status quo (ironically enough,
more firmly in Scotland than England)[26] – just in time to allow the
creation of a united front as first the American, then the French,
Revolutions shook the foundations of Britain's *ancien régime*. In
Ireland it occurred essentially when a better option beckoned. Just
as the support of Catholic, Bourbon France for the exiled Stuarts
had at one time made them the last, best hope of serving the
Catholic and peasant cause in Ireland, so nationalist republicans

naturally replaced them when Jacobin atheists took control of England's ancient enemy.

Notes

1 McLynn, *Jacobites*, 131–3; *Eighteenth-Century Ireland*, pp. 629–44; J. Prebble, *Culloden*, repr. 1974, p. 121.

2 See, for example, the generosity the Scottish (and largely pro-Jacobite) community in Gothenburg showed toward their distressed countrymen after the '45: G. Behre, 'Jacobite refugees in Gothenburg after Culloden', *Scottish Historical Review*, LXX, 1991, pp. 58–63.

3 *Early Modern Ireland*, pp. 593–4, 613–14, 615–24.

4 *Eighteenth-Century Ireland*, pp. 629, 644, 647–9; McLynn, *Jacobites*, pp. 136, 137–9.

5 Turner, *James II*, p. 500. Cf. Jones, *Main-Stream*, pp. 35–6.

6 See for example: Hopkins, *Glencoe*, p. 317; *Affairs of Scotland*, pp. 107, 129, 174–5; *Letters of George Lockhart of Carnwath*, p. 314: Lockhart to Walpole, Aix-la-Chapelle, 23 August 1727 ns.

7 For examples of which see: *Jacobite Threat*, p. 116; Blairs Letters 1/120/14: Thomas Codrington to Thomas Innes, St Germain, 21 August 1689; Jones, *Main-Stream*, pp. 66–7 (Middleton); *Lockhart Papers*, II, pp. 336–7.

8 J. Macky, *Memoirs of the Secret Services of John Macky, Roxburghe Club*, 1895, *passim*; *Letters of George Lockhart of Carnwath*, p. 294.

9 E. Gregg, 'The politics of paranoia', in Cruickshanks and Black, *Jacobite Challenge*, pp. 42–4, 51–2.

10 McLynn, *Jacobites*, pp. 130, 135–6.

11 H. Kamen, *Spain 1469–1714. A Society of Conflict*, repr. 1986, p. 264; C. Duffy, *Frederick the Great. A Military Life*, 1985, pp. 103–8, 174–7.

12 McLynn, *Jacobites*, pp. 137–9.

13 Sedgwick, *House of Commons*, I, p. 77; Colley, *In Defiance*, pp. 271–85.

14 I. R. Christie, 'Party in politics in the age of Lord North's administration', *Parliamentary History*, VI, 1987, pp. 49–62.

15 Monod, *Jacobitism*, pp. 137–8, 144.

16 Monod, *Jacobitism*, p. 293; F. O'Gorman, *The Rise of Party in England. The Rockingham Whigs 1760–82*, 1975, p. 481.

17 P. Jenkins, *The Making of a Ruling Class. The Glamorgan Gentry 1640–1790*, 1983, pp. 152–7, 175–6, 184.

18 Sedgwick, *House of Commons*, II, pp. 25–6; K. G. Feiling, *The Second Tory Party 1714–1832*, 1951, p. 73.

19 Monod, *Jacobitism*, p. 220, and see for example, *Autobiography of Samuel Bamford*, pp. 19–20, 22. The same tendency may have been present among plebeian Scots Jacobites: Pittock, *Invention of Scotland*, pp. 79, 100.

20 Prebble, *Culloden*, pp. 143–307 *passim*.

21 B. Lenman, *The Jacobite Clans of the Great Glen 1650–1784*, 1984, pp. 177–9, 188, 190, 194, 197–8.

22 Ibid., pp. 202–3, 206–9.

23 *Eighteenth-Century Ireland*, pp. 404–10.

24 Monod, *Jacobitism*, pp. 110–11.

25 T. Dunne, 'Popular ballads, revolutionary rhetoric and politicisation', in H. Gough and D. Dickson, eds., *Ireland and the French Revolution*, Dublin, 1990, pp. 141, 147; T. Bartlett, 'Defenders and Defenderism in 1795', *Irish Historical Studies*, XXIV, 1985, p. 388.

26 Colley, *Britons*, pp. 124–32.

Conclusion

Apart from some eccentric late Victorian posturing, the death of Henry 'IX' signalled the end of Jacobitism, and with it the last of Britain's dynastic wars.[1] At this point it is therefore appropriate to ask a devastating, but simple, question. So what?

For nearly seventy years Jacobitism was the mortal enemy of the prevailing political order in the British Isles. Over the course of time it became the natural vehicle for the expression of hostility to that order. Yet in some important ways it acted to soften the expression of such discontents from the point of view of the beneficiaries of the political status quo. Because Jacobitism was ultimately a traditional, conservative movement in social terms – its leaders were always drawn from among the customary leaders of British society – the social resentments moving many of its plebeian adherents were safely muffled. If there was one thing patrician Whigs and Jacobites could agree on, it was the need to maintain order. Thus while Jacobitism became, *de facto*, a radically tinged political movement (see document 7), there was never any danger of a reign of terror in the event of a Jacobite victory. From a social point of view Jacobitism was *safe*, as perhaps more than one old Whig grandee may have wistfully recalled during Britain's late-eighteenth-century confrontations with American Patriots and French Jacobins. Therein, too, may lie its enduring appeal for the primarily middle-class readers of popular romances on the subject.

The grisly fate of so many Jacobites may too have encouraged the next couple of generations of political dissidents in England and

Scotland to do their best to stay within the bounds of conventional, constitutional politics. For if there was one institution which truly benefited from the Jacobite experience it was the British state. The modern constitutional doctrine that Parliament (and hence those who control it) enjoys absolute sovereignty and authority over the inhabitants of the British Isles – even the right legally to wrong them[2] – was largely constructed as a response to Jacobite appeals to a higher authority. The physical authority of the state also expanded. The standing army more than doubled in size, the fiscal 'sinews of power' were enormously strengthened and the overseas and domestic intelligence network of His Majesty's Government became truly formidable. Some of these advantages were undoubtedly lost in the interlude between the demise of Jacobitism and the rise of Jacobinism, but lingering institutional expertise and the certain knowledge that military coercion, spies and the suspension of civil liberties could be both made politically palatable to grumpy back-benchers and prove effective in containing subversive movements, was surely an asset for the authorities in the 1790s.

In other ways too, the British state emerged from the Jacobite era strengthened and empowered. As Linda Colley has convincingly demonstrated in her work on the emergence of a distinctive 'British' patriotism 1707–1837, as much as Jacobitism gave the opponents of the established order a common cause to rally around, it also gave the supporters of the status quo a defining 'Other'. Vehemently Protestant anti-Jacobitism thus became the first touchstone of British patriotism.[3] Ironically, however, if Dr Colley is right, Jacobitism may have also been instrumental in laying the first seeds of the disintegration of the very British patriotism it helped create. For the paranoid Erastianism of the Whig regime, which so weakened the Church of England and set it on the path to political and social marginalisation, stemmed directly from the Whigs' perception of the Church of England as one of the major producers of potential Jacobites. As regards the potential rivals of a 'British' identity, the impact of Jacobitism was, however, more immediately deleterious. Scottish patriotism, which for nearly twenty years after the Glorious Revolution seemed to be building up the potential to challenge English imperial domination of the British Isles, was comprehensively broken 1707–46.[4] It ended the eighteenth century tarred not only by its eventual association, *faute de mieux*, with Jacobitism, but with catastrophic failure. There is both poignancy and significance in the fact that the Scottish Jacobins were basically uninterested in the liberation of 'North Britain'.[5] In Ireland the common interests of the outnumbered Protestant Ascendancy and the powers-that-were in Westminster precluded much kicking at the traces of English control before 1760. After effective Jacobitism had died and a genuine, interdenominational Irish patriotism began to appear, however, the experience of the Jacobite era once again proved useful, and Ireland, like Scotland before it, was bulldozed into a singularly unhappy constitutional union with England.

So if Jacobitism was such a disaster for its adherents, and put such a blight on the prospects of future challenges to the existing political order in the British Isles, who, other than the British state, benefited? The only candidates are Britain's rivals in Europe. Jacobitism survived for as long as it did because various Continental powers encouraged and sustained it. Jacobitism was obviously useful as a latent threat with which to exert pressure on the Whig regime in Britain. Less obviously, contributing to it could also serve as a way of demonstrating a monarch's Catholic piety and support for ideological legitimism.[6] The potency of Jacobitism, and perhaps its major impact on the history of Europe, however, may well lie in the silent threat it posed to the power of Britain's ruling elite for over sixty years. For more than twenty of those years, 1714–35, there was no pan-European war. During that time Russia and Prussia emerged as great powers and the Bourbons revitalised the Spanish empire. To ascribe all this to the Jacobite menace would be ridiculous. Yet by inhibiting British responses to changes that intrinsically upset that shibboleth of British foreign policy: the balance of power (i.e. the maintenance of the status quo), the Jacobites may have facilitated the onset of a rare phenomenon in early modern European history which tends to be much undervalued by late-twentieth-century historians – a sustained period of (relative) peace.

Notes

1 Pittock, *Invention of Scotland*, pp. 120–7.

2 R. J. Frankle, 'Parliament's right to do wrong: the parliamentary debate on the bill of attainder against Sir John Fenwick 1696', *Parliamentary History*, IV, 1985, pp. 71–81.

3   Colley, *Britons*, 1992, p. 25.

4   Lenman, *Jacobite Risings*, p. 285.

5   J. D. Brims, 'The Scottish 'Jacobins', Scottish nationalism and the British union', in R. Mason, ed., *Scotland and England 1286–1815*, Edinburgh, 1987, pp. 247–62. Cf. Murray Pittock's more positive interpretation of the Jacobites' impact on the Scottish national cause, *Invention of Scotland*, pp. 40, 59–60, 82, 84, 117–19, 135–9, 153.

6   Black, *Eighteenth Century*, p. 280.

Illustrative documents

The original spelling and format of these documents has been preserved wherever possible, with alterations made only to clarify the text. Punctuation has been modernised where it elucidates the sense of the letter, and capitalisation has been modernised throughout. All contractions have been silently expanded; other alterations are in square brackets.

1 *Life of James II*, ii. 342–3: James II to the Scottish Convention, 1 March 1689 ns

My Lords and Gentlemen, whereas we have been informed that you, the peers and representatives of shires and boroughs of that our antient kingdom, who are to meet togather at our good town of Edinburgh some time of this instant March, by the usurped authority of the Prince of Orange [William III]; we think fit to let you know, that as we have at all times relyd upon the faithfullness and affection of you, our antient people, so much, that in our greatest misfortunes heretofore, we had recours to your assistance with good success to our affairs, so now again, we require of you, to support our Royal intrest, expecting from you what becomes faithful and loyal subjects; generous and honest men; that will neither suffer your selves to be cojol'd nor frighted into any action, not becomeing true hearted Scotchmen. And that to support the honour of the nation, you will contemn the base example of disloyal men, and eternelize your name by a loyalty sutable to the professions you have ever made to to us; in doing thereof you will chuse the safest part, since thereby you will evite the danger you must needs undergo, the infamy and disgrace you bring upon your selves in this world, and the condemnation due to the rebellious in the next; and you will likewise have the opertunity to secure to yourselves, and your posterity, the gracious promises which we have so often made of secureing your religion, laws, properties and rights, which we are still resolved to performe, as soon as it is possible for us to meet you safely in a Parliament of our antient kingdom: in the mean time fear not to declare for us your lawfull sovereign, who will not fail on our part to give you such speedy and powerfull assistance, as shall not only enable you to defend yourselves from any forreign attempts, but put you in a condition of asserting our right against our enemies, who have depressed the same by the blackest of usurpations, the most unjust as well as most unnaturall attempts, which the almighty God may for a time permit and let the wicked prosper, yet then must bring confusion upon such workers of iniquity; we likewise let you know we shall pardon all such as shall return to their duty before the last day of this month inclusive, and that we shall punish with the rigour of our laws all such as shall stand in rebellion against us or our authority. So, not doubting but that you will declare for us, and suppress whatever may oppose our intrest, and that you will send some of your number to us, with an account of your diligence, and the posture of our affairs, we bid you heartely farewell. Given on board the St Michel, March the first, *anno domini* 1689. By his Majesty's command. Melfort.

2 T. B. Howell (ed.), *A Complete Collection of State Trials* (33 vols., 1816–26), xii. cols. 817–19: Sir John Ashton's final, scaffold, declaration, 28 January 1690

Mr Sherif, Having observed that the methods of making speeches at the place of execution were not always attended with the designed successes; and thinking it better to enjoy my last minutes in devotion and holy communion with my God, I have prepared this paper to leave in your hands, as well to assert my principles as to testify my innocency.

As to my religion, I profess, by God's grace, to die in the faith in the which I was baptized: that of the Church of England, in whose communion (nothing doubting of my salvation through the merits of my saviour) I have always thought myself safe and happy. According to her principles and late much esteemed doctrine (though now unhappily exploded) I have regulated my life; believing myself obliged, by my religion, to look upon my rightful, lawful Prince (whatever his principles were, or his practises might be) as God's viceregent, and accountable (if guilty of maladministration) to God only, from whom he received his power; and always believing it to be contrary to the laws of God, the Church, and the realm, upon any pretence whatsoever, to take up arms against him. And let all the world take notice in this belief I die. But I have more particular obligations to the king, my master, whom I had the honour to serve, and received many signal favours from him, for 16 years past; so that gratitude (a thing not much esteemed at this time) as well as duty and religion, commanded the utmost service I could pay him. And when I add these considerations: that we were born his liege subjects; that we had solemnly professed our allegiance, and often confirmed it with oaths; that his Majesty's usage, after the Prince of Orange's arrival, was very hard, severe, and (I may say) unjust; and, that all the new methods of settling this nation have hitherto made it more miserable, poor, and more exposed to foreign enemies; and, that the religion we pretend to be fond of preserving is now much more than ever likely to be destroyed. There seemed to me no way to prevent the impending evils, and save these nations from poverty and destruction, but the calling home our injured sovereign, who, as a true father of his country, has (notwithstanding all his provocations and injuries) a natural love and tenderness for all his subjects. And I am so far from repining at the loss of my life, that had I ten thousand I should rather think myself obliged to sacrifice them all than omit any just and honest means to promote so good and necessary a work. And I advise and desire all my fellow subjects to think of their duty and turn to their allegiance, before the severe judgments of God overtake them for their perjury and rebellion. But certainly the good and interest of these nations, abstracted from all other considerations, will ere long convince them of the necessity of doing it.

. . . Bless, protect and strengthen, O Lord God, my good and gracious king and master! In thy due time let the virtue, goodness, and innocency of the queen, my mistress, make all their enemies blush, and silence the wicked and unjust calumnies that malice and envy have raised against her. Make her and these nations happy in the Prince of Wales; whom from unanswerable and undoubted proofs, I know to be her son. Restore them all, when thou seest fit, to their just rights, and on such a bottom as may support and establish the Church of England, and once more make her flourish, notwithstanding what she hath received of late from her prevaricating sons. Forgive, forgive, O Lord, all my enemies; bless all my friends; comfort and support my dear afflicted wife, and poor babes; be thou a husband and a father to them; for their sakes only I could have wished to have lived; but pardon that wish, O good God, and take my soul into thy everlasting glory! Amen.

3   Carte 181, ff. 525ar-525br: 'His Majestie's Most Gracious Declaration to all his Loving Subjects', 17 April 1693 ns

Whereas we are most sensible that nothing has contributed so much to our misfortunes, and our people's miseries, as the false and malicious calumnies of our enemies, therefore we have always been, and still are most willing to condescend to such things as after mature deliberation, we have thought most proper for renewing thereof, and most likely to give the fullest satisfaction and clearest prospect of the greatest security to all ranks and degrees of our people, and because we desire rather to be beholding to our subjects' love to us then to any other expedient whatever, for our restoration; we have thought fit to let them know beforehand our royal and sincere intentions; and that whenever our people's united desires, and our circumstances give us the opportunity to come and assert our right, we will come with the Declaration that follows.

James R.

When we reflect upon the calamities of our kingdoms, we are not willing to leave anything unattempted whereby we may reconcile our subjects to their duty, and tho we cannot enter into all the particulars of Grace and goodness which we shall be willing to grant, yet we do hereby assure all our loving subjects that they may depend upon everything that their own representatives shall offer, to make our kingdoms happy. For we have set it before our eyes, as our noblest aim, to do yet more for their constitution, then the most renowned of our ancestors. And as our chiefest interest, to leave no umbrage for jealousie, in relation to religion, liberty and property.

And to encourage all our loving subjects, of what degree or quality soever, to set their hearts and hands to the perfecting of so good a work, and to unite themselves in this only means of establishing the future peace and prosperity of these kingdoms, we have thought fit to publish and declare, that, on our part, we are ready and willing wholly to lay aside all thoughts of animosity or resentment for what is past, desiring nothing more then that it should be buried in perpetual oblivion. And do therefore by this our Declaration under our Great Seal, solemnly promise our free pardon and indemnity to all our loving subjects, of what degree or quality soever, who shall not by land or sea oppose us and those we shall think necessary to accompany our own person, in this just attempt to recover our right. Or (in such a number of days after our landing, as we shal hereafter express) shal not resist them who in any part of our dominions shall according to their duty assert and maintain the justice of our cause. Beseeching God to incline the hearts of our people that all effusion of blood may be prevented, and righteousness and mercy take place. And for that end, we further promise to all such as shall come to, and assist us, that we will reward them according to their respective degrees and merits.

We do further declare that we will, with all speed, call together the representative body of our kingdom. And therein will inform ourselves what are the united interests and inclinations of our people, and with their concurrence, will be ready to redress all their grievances, and give all those securities of which they shall stand in need.

We likewise declare, upon our royal word, that we will protect and defend the Church of England, as it is now established by law. And secure to the Members of it, all the churches, universities, colledges and schools, together with their immunities, rights and priviledges.

We also declare, we will with all earnestness recommend to that Parliament such an impartial liberty of conscience, as they shall think necessary for the happiness of these nations.

We further declare, we will not dispense with, or violate the Test. And, as for the dispensing power in other matters, we leave it to be explained and limited by that Parliament.

We declare also, that we will give our royal assent to all such bills as are necessary to secure the frequent calling and holding of Parliaments: the free elections and fair return of members; and provide for impartial tryals; and that we will ratifie and confirme all such laws, made under the present usurpation, as shall be tendered to us by that Parliament.

And in that Parliament we will also consent to everything they shall think necessary to re-establishing the late Act of Settlement of Ireland, how to recompence such of that nation as have followed us to the last, and who may suffer by the said re-establisment, according to the degree of their sufferings thereby. Yet so as that the said Act of Settlement may alwais remain intire.

And, if Chimny-Money, or any other part of the revenue of the Crown, has been burthensome to our subjects, we shall be ready to exchange it, for any other assessment that shall be thought more easie.

Thus we have sincerely declared our royal intentions, in terms we think necessary, for setling our subjects' minds, and according to the advice and intimations we have received from great numbers of our loving subjects, of all ranks and degrees, who have adjusted the manner of our coming to regain our own right, and to relieve our people from oppression and slavery.

After this, we suppose it will not be necessary to enumerate the tyrannical violations, and burthens, with which our kingdoms have been oppressed, and are now like to be destroyed.

And whereas our enemies endeavour to affright our subjects with the apprehensions of great sums which must be repaid to France, we positively assure them that our dearest brother the Most Christian King expects no other compensation for what he has done for us than meerly the glory of having succor'd an injur'd Prince.

We only add, that we come to vindicate our own right, and to establish the liberties of our people. And may God give us success in the prosecution of the one, as we sincerely intend the confirmation of the other. James R.'

4 *Original Papers*, ii. 385–6: the Old Pretender to Louis XIV, 18 February 1713 ns

Sire, What terms shall I employ to express my gratitude to your Majesty, before I leave the asylum which you have been pleased to grant me, almost ever since I was born, and which you do not permit me to leave, but in order to procure for me another more suitable, in the present state of your affairs and of my own? Words fail me, to express how my heart is penetrated, by the remembrance of your Majesty's benificence and former kindness towards me. The care you are now pleased to take of me, and of whatever concerns me, crowns the whole, and encourages me, in the sad situation I am in, from the confidence I have, in a generosity that has no example for its continuance, in a wisdom which is accustomed to accomplish the greatest designs, and in a bounty which unweariedly extends itself to me and to my family.

It is with all possible earnestness, that I request your Majesty for the continuance of it, towards me and the Queen my mother [Mary of Modena]; the only person who is left of all those who were most dear to me, and who deserves so much of me, as the best of mothers. Besides, she does not fall short of me in the sentiments of gratitude to your Majesty, with which she herself inspired me, from my tenderest infancy.

When I have assured your Majesty of my most sincere and fervent wishes for your prosperity and happiness, I have nothing further to say, but to conjure your Majesty to be thoroughly persuaded, that you will always find in me the respect, attachment, and, if I can presume to say, the tenderness of a son, a will always ready, not only to follow, but even to go before your own in all things, during the time of my exile; and if I shall ever see myself restored to my dominions, a faithful ally, who will make it his glory and his happiness to concur with the first designs of a king who does honour to royalty.

5 *Affairs of Scotland*, pp. 336–41: the Jacobite council at Derby, 5 December 1745

The 4th of December the whole army marched into Derby. The Duke of Devonshire had left the town with his regiment the day before; the Duke's army [i.e. Cumberland's army] were that night at Stafford and the next at Litchfield. [On] The 5th in the morning Lord George Murray and the commanders of battalions and squadrons waited upon the Prince [Charles Edward Stuart], and Lord George told him that it was the opinion of every body present that the Scots had now done all that could be expected of them. That they had marched into the heart of England ready to join any party that would declare for him, that none had, and that the counties through which the army had passed had seemed much more enemies than friends to his cause. That there was no French landed in England, and that if there was any party in England for him, it was very odd that they had never so much as either sent him money or intelligence or the least advice what to do. But if he could produce any letter from any person of distinction in which there was an invitation for the army to go to London, or to any part of England that they were ready to go. But if nobody had either invited them or meddled in the least in their affairs, it was to be supposed that their was either no party at all, or if there was they did not chuse to act with them, or else they would ere now have lett them know it. Suppose even the army marched on and beat the Duke of Cumberland, yett in the battle they must lose some men, and they had after that the King's own army, consisting of 7000 men near London to deal with. On the contrary, if either of these armies beat them, there would not a man escape, as the militia, altho they durst never face the army while in a body, yett they would have courage enough to putt an end to them if they were routed. And so the people that were in arms in Scotland would fall an easy sacrifice to the fury of the government. Again, suppose the army was to slip the King's and Duke's army and gett into London, the success of the affair would intirely depend upon the mobs declaring for or against it, and that if the mob had been much inclined to his cause, since his march into England, that to be sure some of his friends in London would have fallen upon some method to have let him know it. But if the mob was against the affair 4,500 men would not make a great figure in London. Lord George concluded by saying that the Scots army had done their part, that they came into England at the Prince's request to join his English friends, and to give them courage by their appearance to take arms and declare for him publickly as they had done, or to join the French if they had landed; but as none of these things had happened, that certainly 4,500 Scots had never thought of putting a king upon the English throne by themselves. So he said his opinion was they should go back and join their friends in Scotland, and live and die with them, and the French (who at Derby the army learned had landed in Scotland with Lord John Drummond, but did not know their numbers but believed 4,000 men [actually only 700 arrived]). After Lord George had spoke he desired all the rest of the gentlemen present to speak their sentiments, and they all agreed with Lord George except two [the Duke of Perth and Sir William Gordon], who were for going to Wales to see if the Welch would join. It was urged too that Wade's army, which was following, must likewise be fought with as the other two armies would certainly stop the Prince's by fighting or other methods, which would give Wade time enough to come up. The Prince heard all these arguments with the greatest impatience, fell into a passion and gave most of the gentlemen that had spoke very abusive language, and said that they had a mind to betray him. The case was he knew nothing about the country nor had not the smallest idea of the force that was against him, nor where they were situated. His Irish favourites, to pay court to him, had always represented the whole nation as his friends, had diminished much all the force that was against him, and he himself believed firmly that the soldiers of the regulars would never dare fight against him, as he was their true prince. For all the success he had had as yett he attributed to the mens' consciences not allowing them to fight against him, than to the power of the broadsword, and he always believed he should enter St James with as little difficulty as he had done Holyrood house. He continued all that day positive he would march to London. The Irish in the army were always for what he was for, and were heard to say that day that they knew if they escaped being killed the worst that could happen to them was some months' imprisonment. The Scots were all against it; so at night the Prince sent for them and told them he consented to go to Scotland, and at the same time told them that for the future he would have no more councills, for he would neither ask nor take their advice, that he was accountable to nobody for his actions but to his father. And he was as good as his word, for he never after advised with any body but the Irish officers, Messrs [John] Murray [of Broughton] and [John] Hay [of Restalrig] and never more summoned a council.

6 *State Trials*, xix. cols. 739–42: Dr Archibald Cameron's final statement, 6 June 1753

Being denied the use of pen, ink, and paper (except in the presence of one or more officers, who always took away the paper from me whenever I began to write complaints) and not even allowed the use of a knife with which I might cut a poor blunted pencil that had escaped the diligence of my searchers, I have, notwithstanding, as I could find opportunity, attempted to set down on some slips of paper, in as legible characters as I was able, what I would have my country satisfied of in regard to myself, and the cause in which I am now going to lay down my life.

As to my religion, I thank God I die a member (though unworthy) of that church, in whose communion I have always lived, the Episcopal Church of Scotland as by law established before the most unnatural rebellion begun in 1688, which, for the sins of these nations, hath continued to this day: and I firmly trust to find, at the most awful and impartial tribunal of the Almighty king of kings, through the merits of my blessed Lord and Saviour Jesus Christ, that mercy (though undeserved) to my immortal part, which is here denied to my earthly, by an usurper and his faction, though it be well known I have been the instrument of preventing the ruin and destruction of many of my poor deluded countrymen who were in their service. . .

I thank kind providence I had the happiness to be early educated in the principles of Christian loyalty, which, as I grew in years, inspired me with an utter abhorrence of rebellion and usurpation, though ever so successful, and when I arrived at man's estate, I had the testimony both of religion and reason to confirm me in the truth of my first principles. Thus my attachment to the royal family is more the result of examination and conviction, than of prepossession and prejudice; and as I am now, so was I then, ready to seal my loyalty with my blood. As soon therefore as the royal youth [Charles Edward] had set up the king, his father's, standard, I immediately, as in duty bound, repaired to it. And as I had the honour, from that time, to be almost constantly about his person till November 1748 (excepting the short time after the affair of Culloden, that his Royal Highness was in the Western Isles) I became more and more captivated with his amiable and princely virtues, which are indeed in every instance so eminently great, as I want [i.e. lack] words to describe.

I can farther affirm (and my present situation, and that of my dear prince too, can leave no room to suspect me of flattery) that as I have been his companion in the lowest degree of adversity that ever prince was reduced to, so I have beheld him too, as it were, on the highest pinnacle of glory, amidst the continual applauses, and I had almost said, adorations of the most brilliant court in Europe; yet he was always the same, ever affable and courteous, giving constant proofs of his great humanity, and of his love for his friends and his country. What great good to these nations might not be expected from such a prince, were he in possession of the throne of his ancestors! And as to his courage, none that have ever heard of his glorious attempt in 1745, can, I should think, call it in question.

. . .I thank God I was not in the least daunted at hearing the bloody sentence, which my unrighteous judge pronounced with a seeming insensibility, till he came to these words 'But not till you are dead', before which he made a pause, and, uttering them with a particular emphasis, stared me full in the face, to see, I suppose, if I was as much frightened at them, as he, perhaps, would have been had he been in my place. As to the guilt he said I had to answer for, as having been instrumental in the loss of so many lives, let him and his constituents see to that. At their hands, not at mine, will all the blood that has been shed on that account be required.

God, of his infinite mercy, grant they may prevent the punishment which hangs over their heads, by a sincere and timely repentence, and speedy return to their duty.

I pray God to hasten the restoration of the royal family (without which this miserably divided nation can never enjoy peace and happiness) and that it may please him to preserve and defend the King, the Prince of Wales, and the Duke of York, from the power and malice of their enemies; to prosper and reward all my friends and benefactors, and to forgive all my enemies, murderers and false accusers from the Elector of Hanover [George II] and his bloody son [Cumberland], down to Samuel Cameron, the basest of their spies, as I freely do from the bottom of my heart.

7 Stuart Papers 345/164: Charles Edward Stuart's notes for points to be included in his next declaration, 1753

1st. The Parliament to be annual or at most triannual.
2nd. The number of persons in offices both civil and military capable to sit in the House of Commons not to exceed fifty.

3rd. When all is quiet to disband the standing army and establish a national millitia in their place.

4th. The liberty of the press to be confirmed.

5th. To strive to remove all abuses that may be in the power given to the civil ministers.

6th. To assert the rights of the people to withstand the encroachments of power destructive to their religious or civil rights.

7th. An union between the three kingdoms to be proposed to a free Parliament.

8th. To mention my religion, which is of the Church of England as by law established, as I have declared myself when in London the year 1750.

8 *Affairs of Scotland*, pp. 148–9: Lord Elcho's account of the English Jacobites' final severing of relations with Charles Edward Stuart (1754)

The partisans of the Prince [Charles Edward] in England at that time granted him a pension of 5000 pounds sterling a year. One gentleman, [James] Dawkins [MP] by name, gave a thousand of the five. All of this money was this year taken away from him for ever, and all these gentlemen became his enemies and particularly this same Dawkins. They had sent one of their friends [Daniel Macnamara] to persuade the Prince to part with his mistress [Clementina Walkinshaw], because her sister had a place in the service of the Princess of Wales at the court in London, and they feared a correspondence between the two sisters. The Prince replied that he would not put away one of his dogs to please them, and ended by demanding more money, stating that what they gave him was not sufficient. The messenger said to him that these gentlemen were not his bankers, that what they gave him was given out of pure generosity, and that he ought to be more than content. The Prince retorted that he knew the names of all those that had sent him the money, and that if they would not continue to do so, he would send a list of their names to the King of England. All these gentlemen were so indignant at these threats that from that time the Prince never received a halfpenny from England.

9 W. S. Lewis, W. H. Smith, G. L. Lam and E. M. Martz, eds., *Horace Walpole's Correspondence With Sir Horace Mann and Sir Horace Mann the Younger* (48 vols., New Haven, Connecticut, 1971), xxv 100–1: Mann to Walpole, 12 December 1780

. . . I cannot refrain from telling you a story which will make a noise in the world and make you laugh. What France and Spain will say to it I cannot pretend to judge, though their views of giving a Stuart heir to the crown of England will be defeated by what has happened here two days ago by the separation of the Countess Albany [Louise von Stolberg] from her husband [Charles Edward]. You know undoubtedly the extravagance of his behaviour, which has of late manifested itself in his cruel and indecent treatment of his wife. On St Andrew's day, which he always celebrated by an extraordinary dose of wine and stronger liquors, he used her extremely ill, and at night committed the most nauseous and filthy indecencies from above and below upon her, tore her hair, and attempted to throttle her. Her screams roused the family [i.e. servants], and their assistance prevented any other violence. She is supposed then to have taken the resolution of leaving him, but strictly concealed it till she could inform Cardinal York of it and receive his answer. His reply was compassionate but exhorting her to bear with his brother's behaviour as long as possible, promising her, however, both protection and assistance in case of need. She made her case privately known to the Great Duke [of Florence] and then concerted with a lady [a 'Mrs Orlandini'] of her acquaintance the method of putting her resolution in execution, which was admirably well managed. She invited that lady to breakfast with on Saturday morning, as she had often done before, in company with the Count [i.e. Charles Edward], who after proposed to the ladies to go out in the coach, and they conducted him to a sort of convent where men are permitted within the first door. The Count followed, but they shut it in his face, and on his persisting to have it opened, the lady who has the superintendance of that place for the Great Duchess and had orders to be there, came to the grate to tell him that the Countess Albanie had put herself under the Great Duke's protection, and was determined never to cohabit with him again, upon which he went grumbling home, menacing vengeance on all those who had a hand in the affair. He says that he knows that I had given many thousand zecchins to his wife to induce her to give him a potion to render him impotent. He sent his first minister [Count Spada] to the Great Duke to complain of what had passed and to demand his wife, but he received a very unfavourable answer.

Bibliography

Manuscript sources
Bodleian Library, Oxford
  Carte Papers
National Library of Scotland
  Lockhart of Lee and Carnwath Estate Papers
  Wodrow Letters
National Library of Wales, Aberystwyth
  Penrice and Margam MSS
  Ottley MSS
Ralph Brown Draughon Library, Auburn University
  Stuart Papers microfilm
Scottish Catholic Archives, Edinburgh
  Blair Letters

Printed primary sources
Atterbury, F., *English Advice to the Freeholders of England*, 1714.
Aufrere, A., ed., *The Lockhart Papers*, 2 vols., 1817.
Bamford, S., *The Autobiography of Samuel Bamford, Volume One: Early Days, Together with an Account of the Arrest &c*, ed. W. H. Chaloner, 1967.
Blaikie, W. B., ed., *Origins of the Forty-Five and Other Papers Relating to That Rising*, Edinburgh, repr. 1975.
Browning, A., ed., *Memoirs of Sir John Reresby*, Glasgow, 1936.
Buckley, E., ed., *Memoirs of Thomas, Earl of Ailesbury. Written by Himself*, Roxburghe Club, 1890.
Charteris, E., ed., *A Short Account of the Affairs of Scotland in the Years 1744, 1745, 1746. By David Lord Elcho*, Edinburgh, 1907.

Clark, J. C. D., ed., *The Memoirs and Speeches of James, 2nd Earl Waldegrave, 1742–63*, 1988.

Clarke, J. S., ed., *The Life of James the Second, King of England, &c, Collected out of Memoirs Writ of His Own Hand*, 2 vols., 1816.

Lenman, B., and Gibson, J. S., *The Jacobite Threat: England, Scotland, Ireland, France: a Source Book*, Edinburgh, 1990.

Gilbert, J. T., ed., *A Jacobite Narrative of the War in Ireland, 1688–1691*, Shannon, repr. 1971.

Hogau, J., ed., *Negociations de M. Le Conite D'Avaux en Irlande 1689–90*, Irish Manuscripts Commission, Dublin, 1934.

Lonsdale, R., ed., *The New Oxford Book of Eighteenth-Century Verse*, Oxford, 1987.

Macky, J., *Memoirs of the Secret Services of John Macky*, Roxburghe Club, 1895.

Macpherson, J. J., ed., *Original Papers; Containing the Secret History of Great Britain from the Restoration to the Accession of the House of Hannover*, 2 vols., 1775.

Macquoid, G. S., ed., *Jacobite Songs and Ballads*, 1887.

Macray, W. D., ed., *Correspondence of Colonel N. Hooke, Agent From the Court of France to the Scottish Jacobites, in the Years 1703–7*, 2 vols., Roxburghe Club, 1870.

O'Kelly, C., 'Macariae excidium or the destruction of Cyprus', in T. C. Croker, ed., *Narratives Illustrative of the Contests in Ireland in 1641 and 1690*, Camden Society, XIV, 1841.

Sedgwick, R., ed., *Some Materials Towards Memoirs of the Reign of King George II, By John, Lord Hervey*, 3 vols., 1931.

Szechi, D., ed., *Letters of George Lockhart of Carnwath, 1698–1732*, Scottish History Society, 1989.

Tayler, A. and H., *Jacobites of Aberdeenshire and Banffshire*, 1928.

Jacobite Letters to Lord Pitsligo, 1930.

True Copies of the Dying Declarations of Arthur Lord Balmerino, Thomas Syddall, David Morgan, George Fletcher, John Berwick, Thomas Theodorus Deacon, Thomas Chadwick, James Dawson, Andrew Blyde, Donald Macdonald Esq, the Rev. Mr Thomas Coppoch, the Rev. Mr Robert Lyon, Edmund Clavering, John Hamilton Esq, James Bradshaw, Alexander Leith, and Andrew Wood, Edinburgh, 1750

Secondary Works

Anderson, M. S., *Europe in the Eighteenth Century 1713/1783*, repr. 1970.

Aubrey, P., *The Defeat of James Stuart's Armada 1692*, Leicester, 1979.

Baxter, S. B., *William III and the Defence of European Liberty 1650–1702*, 1966.

Baynes, J., *The Jacobite Rising of 1715*, 1970.

Bennett, G. V., *The Tory Crisis in Church and State, 1688–1730. The Career of Francis Atterbury, Bishop of Rochester*, 1975.

Black, J., *British Foreign Policy in the Age of Walpole*, Edinburgh, 1985.

Eighteenth Century Europe 1700–1789, New York, 1990.

Bluche, F., *Louis XIV*, transl. M. Greengrass, New York, 1990.

Bossy, J., *The English Catholic Community 1570–1850*, 1976.

Brewer, J., *The Sinews of Power. War, Money and the English State, 1688–1783*, New York, 1989.

Chandler, D., *The Art of Warfare in the Age of Marlborough*, 1976.

Marlborough as Military Commander, 2nd edn, 1979.

Childs, J., *The British Army of William III, 1689–1702*, Manchester, 1987.

The Nine Years War and the British Army 1688–1697. The Operations in the Low Countries, Manchester, 1991.

Clark, J. C. D., *English Society 1688–1832. Ideology, Social Structure and Political Practice During the Ancien Regime*, 1985.

Revolution and Rebellion. State and Society in England in the Seventeenth and Eighteenth Centuries, 1986.

Colley, L., *In Defiance of Oligarchy. The Tory Party 1714–60*, 1982.

Britons. Forging the Nation 1707–1837, 1992.

Cruickshanks, E., *Political Untouchables. The Tories and the '45*, 1979

Dickinson, H. T., *Bolingbroke*, 1970.

Liberty and Property. Political Ideology in Eighteenth Century Britain, 1977.

Duffy, C., *Frederick the Great. A Military Life*, 1985.

The Military Experience in the Age of Reason, 1987.

Feiling, K. G., *The Second Tory Party 1714–1832*, 1951.

Ferguson, W., *Scotland's Relations with England. A Survey to 1707*, Edinburgh, 1977.

Foster, R. F., *Modern Ireland 1600–1972*, 1989.

Fritz, P. S., *The English Ministers and Jacobitism Between the Rebellions of 1715 and 1745*, 1975.

Gibson, J. S., *Playing the Scottish Card. The Franco-Jacobite Invasion of 1708*, Edinburgh, 1988.

Gregg, E., *Queen Anne*, 1980.

Haile, M., *James Francis Edward. The Old Chevalier*, 1907.

Harcourt-Smith, S., *Alberoni, or the Spanish Conspiracy, 1943.*

Hatton, R. M., *Charles XII of Sweden*, New York, 1968.

   George I. Elector and King, 1978.

Hay, D., Linebaugh, P., Rule, J. G., Thompson, E. P. and Winslow, C., *Albion's Fatal Tree. Crime and Society in Eighteenth-Century England*, repr. 1988.

Henning, B. D., ed., *The House of Commons 1660–1690*, 3 vols, 1983.

Hill, B. W., *Robert Harley. Speaker, Secretary of State and Premier Minister*, 1988.

Holmes, G. S., *The Trial of Dr Sacheverell*, 1973.

   British Politics in the Age of Anne, 2nd edn, 1987.

Hopkins, P., *Glencoe and the End of the Highland War*, Edinburgh, 1986.

Horn, D. B., *Great Britain and Europe in the Eighteenth Century*, Oxford, 1967.

Horwitz, H., *Parliament, Policy and Politics in the Reign of William III*, Manchester, 1977.

Jarvis, R. C., *Collected Papers on the Jacobite Risings*, 2 vols., Manchester, 1972.

Jenkins, P., *The Making of a Ruling Class. The Glamorgan Gentry 1640–1790*, 1983.

Jones, G. H., *The Main Stream of Jacobitism*, Cambridge, Massachusetts, 1954.

Kamen, H., *Spain 1469–1714. A Society of Conflict*, repr. 1986.

Kenyon, J. P., *Revolution Principles. The Politics of Party 1689–1720*, 1977.

Langford, P., *A Polite and Commercial People. England 1727–1783*, Oxford, 1989.

   Public Life and the Propertied Englishman 1689–1798, 1991.

Lenman, B., *The Jacobite Risings in Britain, 1689–1746*, 1980.

   The Jacobite Clans of the Great Glen 1650–1784, 1984.

Loades, D. M., *Politics and the Nation 1450–1660*, 3rd, revised, edn, 1986.

Macaulay, T. B., *The History of England From the Accession of James the Second*, ed. C. Firth, 6 vols., New York, repr. 1968.

McLynn, F. J., *France and the Jacobite Rising of 1745*, Edinburgh, 1981.

The Jacobite Army in England, 1745. The Final Campaign, Edinburgh, 1983.

Charles Edward Stuart. A Tragedy in Many Acts, 1988.

Mallet, E., *A History of the University of Oxford, Volume III, Modern Oxford*, 1927.

Michael, W., *England Under George I. The Beginnings of the Hanoverian Dynasty*, Westport, Connecticutt, repr. 1981.

England Under George I. The Quadruple Alliance, 1939.

Miller, J., *James II. A Study in Kingship*, Hove, 1977.

Mitchison, R., *Lordship to Patronage. Scotland 1603–1745*, 1983.

Monod, P. K., *Jacobitism and the English People, 1688–1788*, 1989.

Moody, T. W., Martin, F. X. and Byrne, F. J., eds., *A New History of Ireland, III: Early Modern Ireland 1534–1691*, Oxford, 1976.

Moody, T. W. and Vaughan, W. E., eds., *A New History of Ireland, IV: Eighteenth Century Ireland*, Oxford, 1986.

Namier, L. B., *The Structure of Politics at the Accession of George III*, repr. 2nd edn, 1982.

England in the Age of the American Revolution, repr. 2nd edn, 1970.

O'Gorman, F., *The Rise of Party in England. The Rockingham Whigs 1760–82*, 1975.

Owen, J. B., *The Rise of the Pelhams*, 1957.

Parker, G., *The Military Revolution. Military Innovation and the Rise of the West, 1500–1800*, 1988.

Petrie, Sir Charles, *The Jacobite Movement*, 1st edn, 1932.

The Marshal Duke of Berwick, 1953.

Pittock, M. G. H., *The Invention of Scotland. The Stuart Myth and the Scottish Identity, 1638 to the Present*, 1991, p. 34.

Plumb, J. H., *The Growth of Political Stability in England 1675–1725*, repr. 1977.

Prebble, J., *The Darien Disaster*, 1968.

Culloden, repr. 1974.

Richards, E., *A History of the Highland Clearances. Agrarian Transformation and the Evictions 1746–1886*, 1982.

Riley, P. W. J., *The Union of England and Scotland*, Manchester, 1978.

King William and the Scottish Politicians, Edinburgh, 1979.

Rule, J., *Albion's People. English Society, 1714–1815*, 1992.

Scott, Sir Walter, *Waverley; or, 'Tis Sixty Years Since*, ed. C. Lamont, Oxford, 1981.

Sedgwick, R., ed., *The House of Commons 1715–54*, 2 vols., 1970.

Simms, J. G., *Jacobite Ireland 1685–91*, 1969.

Smith, L. B., *Spain and Britain 1715–1719. The Jacobite Issue*, 1987.

Somerville, D. H., *King of Hearts. Charles Talbot, Duke of Shrewsbury*, 1962.

Speck, W. A., *Tory and Whig. The Struggle in the Constituencies*, 1970.

   The Butcher. The Duke of Cumberland and the Suppression of the '45, 1981.

   Reluctant Revolutionaries. Englishmen and the Revolution of 1688, 1988.

Symcox, G., *The Crisis of French Naval Power, 1688–97*, 1974.

Szechi, D., *Jacobitism and Tory Politics 1710–14*, Edinburgh, 1984.

Tayler, A. and H., *1715. The Story of the Rising*, 1936.

Thompson, E. P., *Customs in Common*, New York, 1991.

Tomasson, K. and Buist, F., *Battles of the '45*, repr. 1978.

Trevelyan, G. M., *England Under Queen Anne. The Peace and the Protestant Succession*, repr. 1948.

Turner, F. C., *James II*, repr. 1950.

Wilson, A. M., *French Foreign Policy During the Administration of Cardinal Fleury 1726–1743. A Study in Diplomacy and Commercial Development*, Westport, Connecticutt, repr. 1972.

Youngson, A. J., *The Prince and the Pretender. A Study in the Writing of History*, 1985

Articles and Essays

Bartlett, T., 'Defenders and Defenderism in 1795', *Irish Historical Studies*, XXIV, 1985, pp. 373–94.

   'An end to moral economy: the Irish militia disturbances of 1793', in C. H. E. Philpin, ed., *Nationalism and Popular Protest in Ireland*, 1987.

Beddard, R., 'The unexpected Whig revolution of 1688', in R. Beddard, ed., *The Revolutions of 1688. The Andrew Browning Lectures, 1988*, Oxford, 1991.

Behre, G., 'Sweden and the rising of 1745', *Scottish Historical Review*, LI, 1972, pp. 148–171.

   'Jacobite refugees in Gothenburg after Culloden', *Scottish Historical Review*, LXX, 1991, pp. 58–63.

Brims, J. D., 'The Scottish 'Jacobins', Scottish nationalism and the British union', in R. Mason, ed., *Scotland and England 1286–1815*, Edinburgh, 1987.

Bruce, M. W., 'Jacobite relations with Peter the Great', *Slavonic Review*, XIV, 1935–6, pp. 343–62.

Cannadine, D., 'The state of British History', *Times Literary Supplement*, 10 October 1986.

Christie, I. R., 'Party in politics in the age of Lord North's administration', *Parliamentary History*, VI, 1987, pp. 49–62.

Clark, J. C. D., 'On moving the middle ground, the significance of Jacobitism in historical studies', in E. Cruickshanks and J. Black, eds., *The Jacobite Challenge*, Edinburgh, 1988.

Corfield, P. J., 'Class by name and number in eighteenth-century Britain', *History*, LXXII, 1987, pp. 38–61.

Cruickshanks, E., 'Lord Cornbury, Bolingbroke and a plan to restore the Stuarts, 1731–1735', *Royal Stuart Papers*, XXVII, 1986, pp. 1–12.

Dickinson, H. T., 'The October Club', *Huntington Library Quarterly*, XXXIII, 1969–70, pp. 155–74.

Dunne, T., 'Popular ballads, revolutionary rhetoric and politicisation', in H. Gough and D. Dickson, eds., *Ireland and the French Revolution*, Dublin, 1990.

Frankle, R. J., 'Parliament's right to do wrong: the parliamentary debate on the bill of attainder against Sir John Fenwick 1696', *Parliamentary History*, IV, 1985, pp. 71–81.

Gill, C., 'The affair of Porto Novo: an incident in Anglo-Swedish relations', *English Historical Review*, LXXIII, 1958, pp. 47–65.

Goldie, M., 'The roots of true Whiggism', *History of Political Thought*, I, 1980, pp. 195–236.

Gregg, E., 'Was Queen Anne a Jacobite?', *History*, LVII, 1972, pp. 358–75.

'Marlborough in exile, 1712–1714', *Historical Journal*, XV, 1972, pp. 593–618.

'The Jacobite career of John, Earl of Mar', in E. Cruickshanks, ed., *Ideology and Conspiracy. Aspects of Jacobitism, 1689–1759*, Edinburgh, 1982.

'The politics of paranoia', in E. Cruickshanks and J. Black, eds., *The Jacobite Challenge*, Edinburgh, 1988.

Harris, M., 'Print and politics in the age of Walpole', in J. Black, ed., *Britain in the Age of Walpole*, 1984.

Hayton, D., 'The Country interest and the party system', in C. Jones, ed., *Party and Management in Parliament, 1660–1784*, Leicester, 1984.

Holmes, G. S., 'The Hamilton affair of 1711-12: a crisis in Anglo-Scottish relations', *English Historical Review*, LXXVII, 1962, pp. 257–82.

Holmes, G. S. and Jones, C., 'Trade, the Scots and the Parliamentary crisis of 1713', *Parliamentary History*, I, 1982, pp. 47–77.

Hopkins, P., 'Sham plots and real plots in the 1690s', in E. Cruickshanks, ed., *Ideology and Conspiracy: Aspects of Jacobitism, 1689–1759*, Edinburgh, 1982.

Hyland, P. B., 'Liberty and libel: government and the press during the succession crisis in Britain, 1712–16', *English Historical Review*, CI, 1986, pp. 863–88.

Jones, G. H., 'The Irish fright of 1688: real violence and imagined massacre', *Bulletin of the Institute for Historical Research*, LV, 1982, pp. 148–53.

Lenman, B., 'The Scottish episcopal clergy and the ideology of Jacobitism', in E. Cruickshanks, ed., *Ideology and Conspiracy. Aspects of Jacobitism, 1689–1759*, Edinburgh, 1982.

McKay, D., 'The struggle for control of George I's northern policy, 1718–19', *Journal of Modern History*, XLV, 1973, pp. 367–86.

Monod, P., 'Jacobitism and Country principles in the reign of William III', *Historical Journal*, XXX, 1987, pp. 289–310.

'The politics of matrimony: Jacobitism and marriage in eighteenth-century England', in E. Cruickshanks and J. Black., eds., *The Jacobite Challenge*, Edinburgh, 1988.

'Dangerous merchandise: smuggling, Jacobitism, and commercial culture in southeast England, 1690–1760', *Journal of British Studies*, XXX, 1991, pp. 150–82.

Nordmann, C., 'Choiseul and the last Jacobite attempt of 1759', in E. Cruickshanks, ed., *Ideology and Conspiracy: Aspects of Jacobitism, 1689–1759*, Edinburgh, 1982.

Sir Charles Petrie, 'The Elibank plot', *Transactions of the Royal Historical Society*, XIV, 1931, pp. 175–96.

'The Jacobite activities in south and west England in summer 1715', *Transactions of the Royal Historical Society*, II, 1935, pp. 85–106.

Rogers, N., 'Popular disaffection in London during the Forty-Five', *The London Journal*, I, 1975, pp. 5–27.

'Resistance to oligarchy: the City opposition to Walpole and his successors, 1725–47', in J. Stevenson, ed., *London in the Age of Reform*, Oxford, 1977.

'Popular protest in early Hanoverian London', *Past and Present*, LXXIX, 1978, pp. 70–100.

'Popular Jacobitism in provincial context: eighteenth-century Bristol and Norwich', in E. Cruickshanks and J. Black, eds., *The Jacobite Challenge*, Edinburgh, 1988.

'Riot and popular Jacobitism in Early Hanoverian England', in E. Cruickshanks and J. Black, eds., *The Jacobite Challenge*, Edinburgh, 1988.

Sharpe, J. A., '"Last dying speeches": religion, ideology and public execution in seventeenth-century England', *Past and Present*, CVII, 1985, pp. 144–63.

Smith, L. B., 'Spain and the Jacobites, 1715–16', in, E. Cruickshanks, ed., *Ideology and Conspiracy: Aspects of Jacobitism, 1689–1759*, Edinburgh, 1982.

Shoemaker, R. B., 'The London 'mob' in the early eighteenth century', *Journal of British Studies*, XXVI, 1987, pp. 273–304.

Speck, W., 'Whigs and Tories dim their glories', in J. Cannon, ed, ed., *The Whig Ascendancy, Colloquies on Hanoverian England*, 1981.

Symcox, G., 'Louis XIV and the outbreak of the Nine Years War', in R. Hatton, ed., *Louis XIV and Europe*, 1976.

Szechi, D., 'The Duke of Shrewsbury's contacts with the Jacobites in 1713', *Bulletin of the Institute of Historical Research*, LVI, 1983, pp. 229–32.

'The politics of "persecution": Scots Episcopalian toleration and the Harley ministry', in W. J. Sheils, ed., *Toleration and Persecution, Studies in Church History*, XXI, 1984, pp. 275–89.

'The Jacobite theatre of death', in, E. Cruickshanks and J. Black, eds., *The Jacobite Challenge*, Edinburgh, 1988.

'Mythistory versus history: the fading of the Revolution of 1688', *Historical Journal*, XXXIII, 1990, pp. 143–53.

'The Jacobite Revolution settlement 1689–1696', *English Historical Review*, CVIII, 1993, pp. 610–28.

Szechi, D. and Hayton, D., 'John Bulls's other kingdoms: the government of Scotland and Ireland', in C. Jones, ed., *Britain in the First Age of Party 1680–1750. Essays Presented to Geoffrey Holmes*, 1987.

Index

163

Holker, John, 130
Holmes, Geoffrey, 2
Holy Roman Empire, 65, 113, 115
Hooke, Nathaniel (Colonel), 56
Hopkins, Paul, 1–2, 3
Hungary, 88

indefeasible hereditary right, 63–4
indemnity, 31, 144
industrial revolution, 6–7
Innocent XII, 117
international relations in Europe,
    87–90, 138
Inverness, 98
Inverness, Earl of, *see* Hay, John,
    of Cromlix
Ireland, 30, 42–3, 43–4, 45–6,
    47–51, 59, 133–4: moral
    economy, 16; social structure,
    16–17, 18; *see also* Jacobite War
Irish, 24, 92
Irish regiments in foreign service,
    see Wild Geese
Italy, 107, 108, 128

Jacobins, Scots, 138
Jacobite clubs, 37
Jacobite court, 21–2, 30–1, 32,
    54, 56, 61, 73, 90, 104, 105,
    110–11, 117, 119–20: political
    commitments, 62–3, 143–5,
    150–1
Jacobite industries, 25, 37, 56
Jacobites: Catholic, 62–3, 130;
    English, 59–66, 85, 114, 115,
    116, 120, 131, 147, 151; Irish,
    126–7, 128, 133–4, 148; Scots,
    4, 66–73, 85, 112, 116, 127,
    130, 131–2, 146–8
    in exile, 92, 112, 116: external,
    126–30; internal, 130–4
    patrician, 4, 24–6, 116, 127, 136,
    116
    plebeian, 4, 24–6, 127, 128, 133,
    147
    Protestant, 31, 62–3, 118, 128–9

religion of, 26, 141–3, 149–50
social structure, 12–13, 17
Jacobite War, in Ireland, 42–3,
    45–9
Jacobitism
    historiography of, 1–8:
    optimists, 2–4; pessimists, 4–5;
    rejectionists, 5–6
    ideology, 4, 30–8
James II, 8, 30, 32, 37, 42–3, 45,
    46–7, 49, 51, 53, 54, 55, 56, 60,
    61, 63, 88–9, 90, 117–18, 133,
    140, 142, 143–5
Jones, George Hilton, 4
Joseph II, 115

Keith, James (General), 114, 129
Kenmuir, Viscount (William
    Gordon), 76
Kensington Palace, 56
Kent, 55, 102
Kettlewell, John, 31
Killiecrankie, battle of, 44
Kilmarnock, Earl of (William
    Boyd), 23
King, Dr William, 114
Kingston, Earl of (Evelyn
    Pierrepont), 21
Kinsale, 43, 48
Kirke, Percy (Major-General), 46

Lacy, Peter (Field-Marshal), 129
La Hogue, battle of, 52, 55
Lancashire plot, 54
Landen, battle of, 53
Langford, Paul, 1–2, 6
Lansdown, Baron (George
    Granville), 75
Lauderdale, Duke of (John
    Maitland), 69
Law, John, 130
Lawton, Charlwood, 22
Layer, Christopher, 37, 93
Legh, Peter, 131
Lenman, Bruce, 4